D1553892

Pick it Up!

Chan Stories to Inspire

by
Venerable Master Hsing Yun

星雲禪話

© 2018 Buddha's Light Publications, USA Corp.

By Venerable Master Hsing Yun
Translated by Jason Greenberger and Jonathon Ko
Edited by Venerable Miao Hsi and Mark Ragsdale
Book design by Mark Ragsdale
Cover designed by Wilson Yau
Cover Art: 'Chan' One-stroke Caligraphy by
Venerable Master Hsing Yun

Published by Buddha's Light Publications, USA Corp.
3139 S. Hacienda Blvd.,
Hacienda Heights, CA 91745
Phone: 626-961-9876
Fax: 626-961-4321
E-mail: info@blpusacorp.com
Website: www.blpusacorp.com

Protected by copyright under the terms of the International
Copyright Union; all rights reserved. Except for fair use in
book reviews, no part of this book may be reproduced for any
reason byany means, including any method of photographic
reproduction, without permission of the publisher. Printed in
Taiwan.

ISBN: 978-1-944271-34-3
Library of Congress Control Number: 2018937810

Contents

Editor's Notes

This little book contains many of the largest figures of Chinese Chan and Japanese Zen Buddhism, and as the saying goes, "big impact happens in small packages." The gōng'ans in this book are specifically chosen by Venerable Master Hsing Yun and he has provided commentary to offer us a clearer picture of the history and to relate it to our modern life. The stories themselves provide us a glimpse into the lives of these Chan Masters who have devoted themselves to the study of Buddhism, and through these stories we can come to understand their compassion, directness, and sense of humor. It is hoped that you will draw inspiration from this book and "Pick it Up!" often.

Mark Ragsdale

Acknowledgements

We would like to take this opportunity to thank the many people who contributed to this project of Buddha's light Publications. We especially appreciate the efforts of Venerable Tzu Jung, President of Buddha's Light Publications, and Executive Director, Venerable Miao Hsi. Special thanks to Fo Guang Shan International Translation Center's Executive Director, Venerable Yi Chao, for her invaluable advice and assistance. We would also like to thank Venerable Hui Dong, Abbot of Hsi Lai Temple, for his support and leadership. We would also like to thank Venerable Miao Hsi and Cherry Lai; Robin Stevens and Wilson Yau for editing and book design. Photos are courtesy of Fo Guang Shan Hsi Lai Temple and our appreciation also goes to everyone who has supported this project from conception to completion.

Pick it Up!

Chan Stories to Inspire

by
Venerable Master Hsing Yun

星雲禪話

One Lettuce Leaf

There were three famous Chan masters from the history of Chan Buddhism who lived during the Tang dynasty. They are Chan Master Xuěfēng Yìcún, Chan Master Yántóu Quánhuò, and Chan Master Qīnshān Wénsuì. These three masters often traveled together.

One day, the three masters had wandered until they were tired and hungry. They went in search of a village where they could beg for alms. By chance, they arrived at a riverbed where a single lettuce leaf was floating down the river.

Chan Master Qīnshān remarked, "Look! There is a leaf of lettuce in the river. If we keep traveling upstream, there are sure to be people living nearby. Let's keep going. I'm confident we'll find a house that will feed us."

Chan Master Yántóu added, "Did you notice how fresh that leaf of lettuce was? It looked unspoiled. What a shame it is that someone just let it flow down the river!"

Chan Master Xuěfēng joined in, "The villagers upstream probably don't care that much about such resources, and don't give it a passing thought to let perfectly good lettuce leaves flow down the river. They might not know how to cherish what they have. Such people are undeserving of us teaching them the Dharma, and likewise unworthy of us begging for alms. Maybe we should go to another village to teach the Dharma and collect alms!"

As the three masters were going back and forth on this topic, they saw someone racing down the riverside.

The man saw the three Chan masters and hurriedly asked, "Masters, may I please ask: have you seen a lettuce leaf float down this river? Just now I was washing lettuce and accidentally lost a leaf. I have to find it quickly. If I lost it that would be a shame."

Hearing this, the three masters laughed heartily, "The people here really cherish what they have. They truly have an affinity with Buddhism. Let us go to where he came from and teach the Dharma."

One lettuce leaf is worth little, but the Chan masters were not looking at its material value. They were considering its value in the minds of others. When Chan masters see a flower or a tree, they are looking at the entire world. In a grain of sand or a stone, they see the billion-fold universes. Although these objects are of little material value, if we can treasure them, we are truly blessed. Is there anything in this world that is not valuable?

A Drop Moistens the Universe

Ōhara Yūgaku was the leader of the agricultural reformation movement during the Tokugawa Period in Japan. His contribution towards the reformation of Japanese agricultural villages was considerable. At age twenty-seven, Ōhara Yūgaku moved to study at Matsuo Temple in Ōmi Province (present day Shiga Prefecture). As soon as he entered the temple, he was lead to the kitchen and assigned the task of washing rice.

One day, Monk Teisō went into the kitchen. He suddenly shouted "Oh the depravity! Come and look at this."

Ōhara Yūgaku quickly stopped the work he was doing and ran over to Monk Teisō, who was pointing to the washing basin. Monk Teisō quipped, "See! You see? When you were washing the rice, this grain fell into the basin. That was incredibly wasteful of you! You have committed a transgression!"

Ōhara Yūgaku wiped some sweat from his brow. He had no idea what to say.

"It's just a grain of rice, right?" Monk Teisō waved his hand and remarked, "Bring over the abacus!"

Ōhara Yūgaku hurriedly borrowed an abacus which he carried back and handed to Monk Teisō.

"One grain of rice can grow into twenty four sprouts which in turn can be used to grow twenty four paddies, and every paddy could be used to produce three hundred clusters of rice flowers." Monk Teisō handed the abacus back to Ōhara Yūgaku and continued, "Here, you add it up.

Once the clusters have been reaped, how many grains of rice would there be?"

"7,200."

"If those thousands of grains were planted, then by during the next harvest in autumn, how many grains of rice would there be?"

"51,840,000."

"Then after three years?"

"Huh?"

"What about after four years or five years?"

"Ummm..."

Ōhara Yūgaku furiously slid beads back and forth on the abacus. Sweat beaded on his brow, dripping down onto his face.

"Where did you think a single grain of rice comes from? If you don't understand even this, you've lived your life in vain!" Monk Teisō picked up the grain of rice from the basin and declared, "This grain of rice was able to get this big because a farmer cared for it. If you cannot awaken to the truth behind a grain of rice and do not give rise to a thought of gratitude, then you are less than human!"

"Here," Monk Teisō placed that grain of rice in Ōhara Yūgaku's hand and concluded, "A drop moistens the universe. Do you understand?"

The philosophy of Chan is a fusion of all forms of Buddhism. The Flower Adornment Sūtra states that one grain of sand or a single pebble both contain the entire trichiliocosm. A ksana lasts as long as an innumerable, unlimited, and incalculable continuity of kalpas. Consequently, all myriad phenomena in this world are buta grain of rice. How could one count them all on an abacus? All phenomena from all the realms originate from the mind!

Monk Teisō wanted Ōhara Yūgaku to undersand the principle of "buddhas see a single grain of rice as though it is as large as Mount Sumeru." To awaken to the Way via a single grain of rice; his teaching is a remarkable elucidation of the Dharma!

One Rest and Five Rests

One day, someone asked Japanese Zen Master Ikkyū Sōjun, "Master, out of the many possible Dharma names, why were you named Ikkyū (one rest)?" Hearing this, Zen Master Ikkyū just replied, "With 'one rest,' all myriad affairs are brought to rest. Is this not an excellent Dharma name?"

The devotee answered, "So it means that 'with one rest, all myriad affairs are brought to rest.' Yes, that is an excellent name."

Zen Master Ikkyū continued, "Actually, one rest isn't enough. It takes two rests."

Wondering, the devotee asked, "How is it that it takes two rests?" Zen Master Ikkyū responded, "Only after birth is brought to rest and death is brought to rest is one able to gain liberation from birth and death. Consequently, worries need to be brought to rest and nirvāṇa needs to be brought to rest. The two need to be brought to rest together."

After hearing this, the devotee understood, and followed up saying, "That's right! It takes two rests."

Zen Master Ikkyū spoke further, "After you've achieved two rests, you should try for three rests."

Astonished, the devotee asked, "What's so good about three rests?"

Zen Master Ikkyū replied, "You know how your wife argues with you every day as though she's a tigress? Well, the best thing would be to divorce her. And, government officials often have to ingratiate themselves to others, and doing that is quite tiring. It's often best for officials to leave their post. In life, there are often disputes. It is best to bring these disputes to a rest. If you can bring your wife, your work, and your disputes all to a rest, then you are experiencing true happiness in the three rests."

The devotee heard this and felt it was correct. He responded, "That's true! Three rests are wonderful."

Zen Master Ikkyū continued, "The best, however, is four rests." The devotee asked, "What are these four rests?"

Zen Master Ikkyū replied, "Bring a rest to alcohol, lust, wealth, and anger. If these four could all be brought to a rest, wouldn't that be great?"

The devotee heard this and nodded in agreement.

Finally, Zen Master Ikkyū concluded, "In truth, even after bringing these four to a rest, it is still not enough, it takes five rests. The most painful thing in life is that our stomachs require us to eat rice, vegetables, and drink water. Our five main internal organs have needs. Fulfilling these needs brings us suffering every day. If all the five internal organs can be brought to rest, all toils will cease to exist."

Zen Master Ikkyū and this devotee began with a discussion of names, starting with Ikkyū meaning one rest through five rests, to reflect upon the nature of life. While one desires this thing or that, nothing can be brought to rest. A thousands rests or ten thousand rests would never compare to a single true rest. With one true rest, all myriad affairs are brought to rest, one will no longer create hostility. This is the Chan of one rest.

One Phrase

Chan Master Nányuán Dàomíng was a native of Yuánzhōu (present day Yíchūn, Jiāngxī) and a student of Chan Master Mǎzǔ Dàoyī. He specialized in using concise speech to connect with and guide practitioners.

One day, Chan Master Dàomíng entered the Dharma hall and proclaimed, "Fast horses only need one lashing, and fast humans only need one phrase. Everyone here in attendance: if you have something to say, please stand up. If you do not have any issues to discuss, then I wish you well."

After Chan Master Dàomíng left the meditation hall, a novice monk who was unable to understand this teaching went to Chan Master Dàomíng and asked him, "Is there something to this 'one phrase' thing?"

Chan Master Dàomíng stuck out his tongue and then said, "Wait until I have attained the characteristic of a wide, long tongue, then I'll tell you."

Afterwards, Chan Master Dòngshān Liángjià came to pay Chan Master Dàomíng a visit. Chan Master Dàomíng entered the Dharma hall and then addressed Chan Master Dòngshān Liángjià, saying, "We already met." Finishing this phrase, he left the Dharma hall.

The next day, Chan Master Dòngshān Liángjià once again asked Chan Master Dàomíng, "Chan Master, I am indebted to you for your compassionate instruction yesterday. However, this student is still unclear. Where was it that Chan Master and I met?"

Chan Master Dàomíng replied, "There is no disconnection between minds, there is a constant flow into the ocean of self-nature."

Chan Master Dòngshān Liángjià replied, "I almost missed that." After that, he bid Chan Master Dàomíng farewell.

Before his departure, Chan Master Dàomíng instructed him: "Study more Dharma and make many friendships."

Chan Master Dòngshān Liángjià asked back, "I will not ask you about your first phrase, but how should I go about making many friendships?"

Chan Master Dàomíng replied, "One phrase is enough."

Afterwards, Chan Master Dòngshān Liángjià always pursued this phrase "make many friendships" when he propagated the Dharma. In the end, he realized that "make many friendships" was actually the Dharma.

Practicing Dharma is of no use unless it is applied and does not need to be excessive or complicated. That would not be practical! Although "make many friendships" is just a single phrase, but if one actually succeeds at it, would that not be the practicing of Dharma? Even if one spoke about the entire twelve sections of the Buddhist Canon but failed to make many friendships, what good would that be?

Defeated by Common Sense

Long ago, Japan had a *Vinaya* Master who was deeply committed to his studies. Known as *Vinaya* Master Gōchō, he heavily emphasized the importance of upholding the precepts. He would frequently travel to various temples in the Kyūshū region and debate the monastic communities on issues related to the precepts. He had never lost a debate, and consequently, no matter which monastery he selected for a visit, once word got out that he was on his way, everyone felt rather uncomfortable.

One time, the abbot of a temple was informed that *Vinaya* Master Gōchō wished to visit his temple. The abbot rushed over to Zen Master Sengai and pleaded for his help. Zen Master Sengai had no intention of refusing, and responded by eagerly pledging his assistance.

When the day arrived, from inside and outside the courtyard, corridors, and even railings an excited crowd had emerged to watch the showdown.

Zen Master Sengai stood at the temple gates with his palms together and greeted *Vinaya* Master Gōchō. "Welcome! Please come in!" He then led him to the courtyard. Although *Vinaya* Master Gōchō arrived on scene high-spirited and confident, once he saw what was written on the courtyard grounds, his face went pale, and without a word he turned to leave as quickly as possible.

The crowd was now in an uproar, but nobody knew what had happened. Everyone was talking about the incident and trying to figure it out. From within the crowd, somebody loudly asked, "*Vinaya* Master Gōchō has a reputation as a gifted orator. Why did he leave before the debate even started?" Another spectator called out, "Zen Master, what exactly was it that you said to him? How come we didn't get to see anything? Why did he just walk away?"

Zen Master Sengai grinned as he pointed to the words he had written. "Look for yourselves!"

They saw that on the ground he had written, "Gōchō, everyone around you wants to kill you. You'd better run while you still can!" The whole temple burst into laughter.

Although Zen Master Sengai had played a mischievous practical joke, everyone still felt that *Vinaya* Master Gōchō turned out to be less than fearless. They could see that while *Vinaya* Master Gōchō normally lectured on the monastic precepts, in reality, he did not have much in the way of common sense.

The monastic precepts are rigid and dogmatic. If you require everyone to conform to them, there will hardly be anyone who can perfectly observe such idealism. Chan contains a spirit of liberation. "Scolding the Buddha and blaming masters" is ubiquitous. These phenomena cannot be properly examined through conventional thinking. In actuality, many of those Chan practitioners who scold the Buddha and blame masters are, in truth, those who genuinely honor the Buddha and Buddhist masters. For instance, Chan Master Dānxiá Tiānrán famously said, "bring some more Buddha statues to burn as firewood" or Chan Master Yúnmén Wényǎn's suggestion that had he been present to hear the baby Buddha proclaim that "on the earth and in heaven, only I am worthy of veneration," he would have "killed him with one blow of my staff and fed him to the dogs." These statements sound like heresy, but in reality, they were smashing idolatrous notions and allowing people to see the true body of the Tathāgata in themselves.

He Came Because It Was Here

Chan Master Yàoshān Wéiyǎn was a native of Shānxī whose family name was Hán. At age seventeen, he became a monk studying with Chan Master Xīshān Huizhao at his temple. Later in life he gained a discreet realization of the Dharma and awakened while under the guidance of Chan Master Shítou Xīqiān. Then, during a visit with Chan Master Mǎzǔ Dàoyī he experienced a great and deep awakening. At age forty-one, he entered Mount Yào in Húnán province to take on students. He thereby became known as Chan Master Yàoshān.

One day, a student monk asked him for instruction: "I have yet to understand the great matter of life and death. Please teacher, in your great compassion, give me guidance on this matter."

Chan Master Yàoshān just answered, "It is not difficult for me to speak a few words regarding this matter. If you are able to appreciate it, that's beneficial, but if my words cause your thoughts to grow and multiply, then I would have committed a transgression. So it would be better off for us to have just never spoken of it at all. That way we could avoid dragging each other down."

The student monk still refused to drop the issue and asked further, "Before Bodhidharma came here to China, did our Eastern land have his intent?"

Chan Master Yàoshān replied, "It did."

The monk then asked, "Given that our Eastern land held his intent, what more was there for Bodhidharma to come here and do?"

Chan Master Yàoshān answered, "He came because it was here."

The monk continued, "Chan Master, you ordinarily do not let student monks read *sutras*. So why is it that you yourself read *sutras* every day?"

Chan Master Yàoshān answered, "I just use them in the hope that I can cover my eyes for a bit, but if I were you, even the thickness of cowhide cannot cover your eyes."

The monk asked Chan Master Yàoshān to give a Dharma talk. Chan Master Yàoshān took his seat on the platform, he said not a single phrase, and simply descended from the platform.

The monk asked, "Chan Master, why did you descend from the platform without having spoken?"

Chan Master Yàoshān replied, "For the *sutras* there are *sutra* masters, for the *sastras* there are *sastra* masters, and for the *vinaya* there are *vinaya* masters. How can you hold me responsible?"

After hearing those words, the monk achieved a great awakening.

When Chan Master Yàoshān spoke of sutra masters, sastra masters, and vinaya masters, all of these masters can speak or lecture on their areas of expertise. However, only Chan cannot be lectured on and spoken of. One must distance oneself from language and writing in order to discover the fountainhead of one's own mind.

Chan Master Yàoshān's unique Dharma style was one of being solemn and solitary. He often used simple language to answer his students because he wanted them to experience the profundity that rest beyond words and speech. In Chan, one should seek to awaken to the speech beyond speech; that which is called the "profound words and speech" or the "methods of essence and function." Cutting through delusion, at times requires affirmation and other times, negation. Chan practitioners must go beyond both affirmation and negation, finding a state which one can settle down within.

To Have Only Stolen Once

When Chan Master Fúyuán Shíwū left temple life to wander, he once met a stranger during his travels, and they found themselves to be remarkably likeminded. One day after they had finished talking, they noticed that evening was already quickly upon them. The two decided to stay the night in a nearby inn.

In the middle of the night, Chan Master Shíwū heard a sound coming from inside their room. He asked his companion, "Is it morning already?" His friend answered, "No, it's still the middle of the night."

Chan Master Shíwū thought to himself that his companion was someone who could go exploring in the darkness. Perhaps he was an extremely clever individual. Chan Master Shíwū listened carefully to his companion's movements. He discovered that his companion had slowly walked over next to him. Chan Master Shíwū caught a hold of him and asked, "Who are you exactly?"

His companion realized that there would be no sense in lying. He replied, "I'm sorry. I'm a thief!"

"So you've been a thief all along. How many times have you committed theft in the past?"

"I've been a thief for quite a number of years already. I'm not really clear on exactly how many times I've committed theft."

"How long are you able to maintain your happiness after each theft?"

"That depends on the value of the item that I have stolen. The longest an item has kept me happy was eight days. After that, I am unhappy once more."

"Ah-ha! So you're just a small time thief who goes after little things. Why haven't you tried going after something big?"

The thief thought to himself, "Could Chan Master Shíwū also have experience in theft?" He could not help but ask, "Chan Master, have you also stolen things from people? How many thefts have you committed?"

Chan Master Shíwū answered, "Only once!"

The thief gave Chan Master Shíwū a skeptical look, "You've only stolen once. How could that be possible?"

Chan Master Shíwū answered, "I've only stolen once but I will be able to enjoy what I have stolen for an entire lifetime."

"Could you teach me how you managed to do that?"

Chan Master Shíwū suddenly grabbed the thief's chest and pointed at his heart, "It was this. Do you understand? The boundless treasure is right here. If you spend a lifetime dedicated to this undertaking, you will never lack in your life."

The thief replied, "A part of me understands, but a part of me does not."

Chan Master Shíwū continued to reveal his teaching. The thief was deeply moved by his words and decided to take refuge in Chan Master Shíwū, becoming a Chan practitioner under his guidance.

Why is it that people always greedily take limited valuables which exist outside of themselves? Why do they forget the treasure that exists in their own minds? The treasure which exists in our minds is a resource more enriching than any minerals of the earth. Our minds enable us to become virtuous sages, and enable us to achieve Buddhahood to become a patriarch. Our minds allow us to exit the burning house of transmigration through birth and death. Why is it that people do not explore that which is inexhaustible? Why not explore the limitless treasure which exists in one's own mind?

The Tea Cup Has Died

Zen Master Ikkyū Sōjun of Japan was a renowned monk of the Rinzai School during the Muromachi period. During his youth he exhibited extraordinary intelligence and wisdom.

One day, the novice Ikkyū accidentally broke his master's beloved tea cup, a priceless antique piece. Ikkyū knew he was in big trouble. He thought to himself, "That's it! The master is sure to scold me, probably even beat me." Thinking this, he swiftly swept up the shards of the cup and hid them away.

Sure enough, his master came soon afterwards, having heard the sound of the cup breaking. He asked Ikkyū, "Just now, I heard a crash. Was something broken here?"

Ikkyū played dumb, quickly stepped forward, and asked innocently, "Master, there is a matter which I would like to ask you for instruction."

His master replied, "What is it? Go ahead and ask."

Ikkyū proceeded, "People born into the world and live quite happily. Why do they have to die?"

The master heard this, patted him on the head, and kindly explained, "Foolish child, that is the way of things. Since there is life, there is also death. See, weather cycles through winter, spring, summer, and fall, objects go through formation, subsistence, decay, and extinction. Humans go through birth, aging, sickness, and death. Things decay and die. This is the principle all myriad things are subject!"

After hearing this, Ikkyū was overjoyed and said, "Master, I have some bad news. Your beloved tea cup has died." As he said this, he took out the shards he had hidden and placed them before his master.

As soon as he saw the shards, the master knew that Ikkyū had been naughty and broke his cup. However, he could hardly contradict the words he had just spoken. He could not help but burst into laughter.

During Zen Master Ikkyū's childhood, he was a mischievous child. But although mischievous, he was also very clever. Sometimes he would engage his master in a battle of wits. Such was the case when he broke his master's beloved tea cup. Though he should've been punished, he turned the topic to the matter of life and death. He led his master into a dialectical trap. He waited for his master to tell him that all myriad things undergo formation, subsistence, decay, and extinction and that all things are subject to breaking down. After his master finished explaining, Ikkyū told him that his tea cup "had died." He ensured that his master could not contradict his own teachings, and therefore, had to treat Ikkyū with leniency. Despite Ikkyū's tender age, he was clever, adaptive, and wise, and his anecdote a brilliant example of Zen humor!

Where is Your House?

The *Nāgasena Bhikṣu Sūtra* is a *sutra* filled with wisdom. The majority of it recounts King Miliṇḍa asking Bhikṣu Nāgasena about the Way. Through practicing Chan, Bhikṣu Nāgasena had awakened to the truth. He was eloquent, his words ingenious and wise, and because of this he was respected by King Miliṇḍa.

One day, King Miliṇḍa asked Bhikṣu Nāgasena, "Are your eyes you?"

Bhikṣu Nāgasena laughed and replied, "No."

"Are your ears you?"

"No."

"Is your nose you?"

"No."

"Is your tongue you?"

"No."

"Then is your body really you?" asked King Miliṇḍa.

Bhikṣu Nāgasena answered, "No, the body is just a collection of causes and conditions. These false composites exists as my body, but it is not my true self."

King Miliṇḍa asked further, "Then are you your consciousness?"

"No, that neither."

King Miliṇḍa finally asked, "Since you are not your eyes, ears, nose, tongue, body, or consciousness, then what are you?"

Bhikṣu Nāgasena chuckled lightly and asked back, "Your majesty, are windows a house?"

King Milinda was caught off guard. He hesitantly answered, "No, windows are not a house."

"Are doors a house?"

"No."

"Are bricks and tiles a house?"

"No, they are not a house either."

"Then beds, chairs, beams, and columns must be a house, right?"

"Of course they are not."

Bhikṣu Nāgasena smiled serenely, "Since windows, doors, bricks, tiles, beams, columns, beds, and chairs are not a house and cannot represent this house, then may I please ask, your majesty: where is your house?"

King Milinda suddenly understood.

What was it that King Milinda understood? He realized the truth of the Dharma that "the truth of emptiness due to dependent origination;" land, mountains, rivers, the universe, and all myriad phenomena all come to exist through causes and conditions. Without causes and conditions, nothing would exist. Everything in the world is connected to one another. Nothing in the world exists independently; nothing in the world is unchanging. Everything comes into existence through causes and conditions, and everything ceases to exist through causes and conditions.

Our bodies are the combination of the causes and conditions of the four great elements: earth, water, fire, and wind. Our houses are built by the combination of various causes and conditions. It could be said that we live within the combination of causes and conditions. When the conditions gather, phenomena form; when the conditions disperse, phenomena cease.

If one is able to realize the "empty nature of dependent origination," one can appreciate Chan vistas.

Where Will I Go in the Future?

Japanese Zen Master Daigu Sōchiku was a native of Gifu. At age eleven, he went to Nanzen Temple in Mino City to become a monk. He studied Zen Master Icchū Tōmoku from the Myōshin Temple branch of the Rinzai School, becoming a Zen monk of the Edo period.

One time when he was still in his youth he performed a cremation ceremony for a follower who had passed away. The follower's mother was in a state of extreme grief. When all of the funerary ceremonies had concluded, she approached Master Daigu Sōchiku and asked for an explanation: "Master! My son has died. Where has he gone?"

Zen Master Daigu Sōchiku answered, "He used to recite Amitābha's name with great sincerity and devotion. Of course he has gone to the Pure Land."

The mother pressed, "What about me? Where will I go in the future?"

Zen Master Daigu Sōchiku replied, "You never recite Amitābha's name. Of course you aren't going to the Western Pure Land. You don't recite the Medicine Buddha's name either, therefore you won't be going to the Eastern Pure Land. At the moment, it is uncertain where your causes and conditions will take you!"

The mother said, "You are an individual who has attained the Way. How can you not know the answer to a matter like this?"

Zen Master Daigu Sōchiku responded, "If it is not heaven, it will have to be one of the hells. I am afraid that gaining a life in the human realm is rather difficult!"

The mother asked skeptically, "Is it really that hard to be reborn in the human realm?"

Zen Master Daigu Sōchiku replied, "The *Lotus Sūtra* states that the human form is difficult to attain. Do you still not understand that?"

The Lotus Sūtra *contains an anecdote about how difficult it is to attain human form. "The number of those who possess human form can be likened to mud on a claw, whereas the number of those lacking human form are as common as the rest of soil on the earth." There is also a famous Buddhist analogy that the rarity of attaining human form is like the chance that a blind tortoise would have of finding a floating plank of wood in the ocean with a hole in it, which was the perfect size for the tortoise to fit its head. For a tortoise to find a plank of wood in that matter and then climb on top of it is similar to the rarity of attaining a human form. From this point of view, we can appreciate how incredibly difficult it is to be born as human. Therefore, there is a saying, "The human body is hard to obtain, yet I have obtained it now; the Dharma is difficult to encounter, yet I have encountered it now. If this body is not used to cultivate in this life, till which lifetime would this body be delivered?"*

Chan Buddhism stresses the importance of the present human life. It tells us to cherish our human form and have confidence in establishing ourselves. One should "Point directly to the mind; attaining Buddhahood by seeing true nature." This is the true meaning of Chan!

Dismiss Him to Heaven

Once when Zen Master Ikkyū Sōjun was traveling, it got dark and he spent the night in a farmhouse. Late that night, he was awoken by the sound of crying. It turned out that the master of the neighboring house had died of illness. His whole family was grieving for him. Zen Master Ikkyū spoke to the owner of the house he was staying at, "How unfortunate! Please tell your neighbors that I wish to pray for the deceased."

The deceased was a hunter and fisher. When he was bed-ridden with illness, he was often troubled by the thought of all the negative karma he had accumulated through killing. He would often see fish and shrimp swarming at him and flocks of birds swooping down at him. He had been suffering and in great pain. After Zen Master Ikkyū heard about this, he began praying for the deceased.

After he finished praying, the family members of the deceased requested that Zen Master Ikkyū perform additional rites and write a letter to Yama, King of the Dead. They wished to petition for the deceased to be permitted into heaven. Since the family members of the deceased requested this, Zen Master Ikkyū promised he would do so. He wrote out an inscription on a piece of paper, folded it up, and placed it in the hands of the deceased. He said to the family, "You needn't cry any longer. The deceased can ascend to heaven now."

The family members of the deceased were extremely grateful to Zen Master Ikkyū. However, they were curious. What was it exactly that Zen Master Ikkyū had written?

They unfolded the letter and saw that all that was written on it were the following lines: "The karma from killing accumulated by the deceased is as large as Mount Sumeru. King Yama, I fear that your record keeping could not list all of these offenses. It would probably be best just to dismiss him to heaven."

When the widow saw this, she was greatly distressed. She protested that Zen Master Ikkyū had told *King Yama* that the transgressions committed by the deceased were so numerous that they could not all be recorded.

Zen Master Ikkyū replied, "Madam, do you not admit that your husband's killing karma was as large as Mount Sumeru?"

The wife of the deceased responded, "I admit it, but is there really no way to deliver him?"

Zen Master Ikkyū explained, "My prayer was done to eradicate his negative karma. It was at your request that I went further and wrote a letter to King Yama, making the case that since this person has committed such vast karmic transgressions, it would be easier to just send him to heaven. Doing so would save *King Yama* the inconvenience of recording such a tedious list. Your husband has the letter in hand. He'll definitely go to heaven."

Zen Master Ikkyū's words are truly both the greatest teachings and sharpest satire for people. The negative karma we've accumulated is certain to come back to us. And so as the saying goes "sentient beings fear effects; bodhisattvas fear causes." Such is the truth.

Will the Buddhas Come to Eat?

Prime Minister Péixiū was a famous Tang dynasty lay Dharma protector. He had long been a follower of Buddhism and scholar of the Dharma. During the reign of Tang Emperor Wǔ Zōng, Buddhism suffered from persecution. Prime Minister Péixiū used his influence to protect Buddhism, and once the persecutions ended, within a few short years was instrumental in reviving it.

In his middle age, Prime Minister Péixiū deepened his understanding by becoming vegetarian and reciting *sutras.* He became known as "Great Scholar of Hédōng." He sent his son to a temple to become a monk and authored a manuscript titled, *Universal Inspirations on Generating Bodhi Mind for Monastics and Lay Buddhists.*

Every time Prime Minister Péixiū went to visit a temple, he often arrived when a Dharma service was to be held. He would usually see people busy preparing fruits and vegetarian dishes that were to be offered to all buddhas and bodhisattvas throughout the ten directions.

Prime Minister Péixiū was puzzled. Finally, he asked the monk in charge of the shrine, "Are all the buddhas and bodhisattvas coming here to eat these?"

The monk replied, "Why wouldn't they come? If they didn't, why would we busy ourselves preparing these offerings for them?"

Prime Minister Péixiū followed up by asking, "If they all come to eat the offerings, why have I never seen any of the offerings decrease in any form? How can you claim they have eaten anything?"

The monk replied, "Prime Minister, of course you won't come to eat the offering, however, all the buddhas and bodhisattvas are able to!"

Prime Minister Péixiū did not quite understand what was said. The monk continued his explanation, "All the buddhas throughout the ten directions in the past, present, and future have been, are, and will always be like bees gathering honey. They extract flavors without harming form or fragrance." Prime Minister Péixiū heard these words and was suddenly enlightened.

Most devotees usually offer fruits and vegetarian dishes to the Triple Gem. Some people wonder, "Do all buddhas and bodhisattvas come to eat these offerings?" If one maintains this mindset, then they will not come. There is even a saying, "the gods know one's intentions." If you simply intend to make an offering, then why worry whether the buddhas and bodhisattvas are aware of it? Therefore, there is a saying: "Seek the Dharma with reverence." This is reflected in a gatha of the Diamond Sūtra, "Cut through doubts and give rise to faith." If one's sincere intention is conveyed, then all is fulfilled.

Do Not Give Rise to Craving and Anger

One day, Chan Master Dàxiāng was speaking the Dharma for the community in the Buddha hall. He told the story of Mañjuśrī Bodhisattva manifesting as a poor beggar woman:

One year in Dàfú Língjiù Temple on Mount Wǔtái in Shānxī province, an open Dharma function was being held. At the time, Mañjuśrī Bodhisattva manifested as a young woman dressed in tattered clothing, carrying her two infants with a dog in tow while going for the food offerings.

The abbot offered the young woman three portions of food. Upon receiving food from the abbot, she pointed to the small dog behind her and said, "Great Monk, this dog also needs to be fed!" On hearing this, the abbot was taken aback, however he still managed to give her another portion. The woman spoke again "Great compassionate Monk, I am currently pregnant with another child and he needs to eat too."

Hearing these words, the abbot was unable to contain himself and angrily lashed out, "How can you be so greedy? You come to a temple to beg for food, but make request after request. Psh! The baby in your womb hasn't even been born yet and still needs to eat? You're just greedy, move along!"

After being scolded by the abbot, the young woman leapt into the air. She reverted back to her form as Mañjuśrī Bodhisattva. The dog reverted into Mañjuśrī's blue lion. The two infants reverted into the young Sudhana and a Khotanese King. A misty cloud of five colors pervaded the sky.

Chan Master Dàxiāng stopped at this point in the story and asked the community, "Everyone, what did Mañjuśrī Bodhisattva come for?"

From within the audience a Chan monk loudly replied, "There is no differentiating between the poor and the rich; nobility and lowliness are one and the same."

Chan Master Dàxiāng laughed loudly and recited a *gatha* that was left behind by Mañjuśrī Bodhisattva: "A bitter gourd is bitter to its roots; a sweet melon is sweet to its stem. It is I who manifests throughout the Three Realms, yet the old monk found me detestable."

After he finished reciting the *gatha*, he returned to the abbot's room.

Events within the world should be examined from both points of view. Bodhisattvas have unlimited compassion and inexhaustible strength from their vows. Although the abbot in the story was able to joyfully offer temple food to visitors, he did so within a certain limit. For instance, the young woman wanted an extra serving for the baby she was carrying in her womb. Based on commonsense, this is not something most people would agree to.

In truth though, the old monk scolding her for being greedy was not necessarily wrong. Just as the woman testing the limits of the old monk's compassion was also not to be faulted. Neither the old monk nor the manifestation of Mañjuśrī Bodhisattva should give rise to love or anger for us. This is the attitude that we should have as practitioners.

Déshān Begging for Alms

In Buddhism, Head Cook is the title for those responsible for feeding the community. This includes the preparation of vegetables, water, rice, and performing cooking duties. The work of a Head Cook is complicated and difficult. Since ancient times, many patriarchs and masters of great virtue had served in this position. They tempered their bodies and minds, gained enlightenment, saw their self-nature, became like the mighty dragons and elephants of Buddhism in upholding the true Dharma. Consequently, in Buddhism the saying goes, "All the three thousand buddhas originated in the kitchen."

During the Tang dynasty Chan Master Xuěfēng Yìcún was a prominent student of Chan Master Déshān Xuānjiàn. At that time, he was the Head of Rice, in charge of preparing it for the community.

One day, as Chan Master Xuěfēng Yìcún was in the middle of boiling rice, he saw Chan Master Déshān Xuānjiàn had arrived with alms bowl in hand, so he asked, "The bell has not yet been rung nor has the board been struck; why are you here for food?"

Chan Master Déshān Xuānjiàn astutely replied, "The bell and board do not need to eat, what need is there for bell ringing and board striking?"

Chan Master Xuěfēng Yìcún scooped up some rice and vegetables for Chan Master Déshān Xuānjiàn who then said, "I should go recite the food offering *dhāraṇī* before I eat."

Chan Master Xuěfēng Yìcún asked, "What would you do if the buddhas and bodhisattvas ate all your food before you finished reciting the food offering *dhāraṇī*?"

Chan Master Déshān Xuānjiàn responded, "I can only ask that the buddhas and bodhisattvas provide me one grain of rice to feed my hunger."

Just like that, master and student achieved oneness in thought, leaving behind a wonderful anecdote for future Chan students.

Can a single grain of rice feed a person's hunger? Those who do not understand the Dharma would likely be unsatisfied with even one whole bowl. How then could a single grain of rice feed a person's hunger? For a person who has awakened to the Way, they remember that "The Buddha can see a grain of rice as though it was as large as Mount Sumeru." A Buddhist knows that a grain of rice could come about due to gathering myriad causes and conditions in the universe. Innumerable causes and conditions occurred to deliver it to one's mouth. If one cannot be satisfied even with countless causes and conditions being fulfilled toward this end, then what could lead one to fullness?

The Fortune of Women

In the Tang dynasty, the renowned Chan Master Zhàozhōu Cóngshěn eradicated the suffering of greed, anger, and ignorance since he attained enlightenment. He devoted his life to teach people in accordance with their needs and conditions.

One day, a woman came to Chan Master Zhàozhōu Cóngshěn and lamented, "Alas! We women truly face vast karmic hindrances."

Chan Master Zhàozhōu Cóngshěn looked upon her with a face full of compassion and said, "Tell me, what karmic hindrances women face?"

The woman's brow drooped down as she began to complain, "As children, women are subjected to our parents' harsh discipline. After we grow up and marry, we become controlled by our husbands. As we grow old, we fall under the management of our children."

The more she spoke, the sadder she became. "Chan Master! Take my children for example. The moment I say something, they yell back, 'Mom, stop nagging!' These are truly karmic hindrances!"

Chan Master Zhàozhōu Cóngshěn laughed and waved his hand, saying, "You shouldn't think of it that way. Actually being a woman is a blessing."

Hearing this, the woman's eyes widened in confusion. She asked, "Where is the blessing?"

Hearing her words, Chan Master Zhàozhōu Cóngshěn smiled broadly and said, "Think about it! During childhood, mothers and fathers adore their daughters

As adults, men come to pursue in love; when growing old, children care for and venerate their mothers. There are so many men and women who loath visiting their fathers but enjoy close ties with their mothers. Women enjoy far greater blessings than men!"

What in life is suffering? What is happiness? The world has a nature of duality, possessing both suffering and happiness. Though we may live in happy conditions, our inability to appreciate this can lead to suffering. On the opposite end of the spectrum, when life is difficult and necessities scarce, one suffers. However people with cultivation can bear it as Yán Huí (a disciple of Confucius) described, "Others worry themselves about a single bamboo dish of rice and a single gourd dish of water; I, Huí, do not allow my joy to be affected by it." For him, such days are not considered as suffering.

So one must create joy and happiness for oneself. People's minds are like factories. Bad factories produce smog or sludge; good factories produce all sorts of fine products depending on the skills of a craft. It was said, "The mind is like a skillful painter who can paint all worlds; the three realms are only in the mind, and all phenomena are only consciousness." Cultivation is cultivating the mind because everything is produced by the mind!

A master of both human affairs and universal principles, Chan Master Zhàozhōu Cóngshěn helped the woman realize that she need not lament over her condition. She need only change her perspective to transform negative into positive, so that a different vista can be realized.

The world may be the same, but one's feelings become different. Changing one's mind in this manner is one of Chan's most skillful Dharma methods.

The Way of Nurturing

A devotee was paying his respects to the Buddha in the main shrine and decided to take a stroll through the monastery's garden. He came across the head gardener who was engrossed in landscaping work. The gardener was trimming the foliage with shears and repotting. He also watered and fertilized withering branches, tending to them with special care.

Puzzled, the devotee asked, "Why do you cut away at perfectly healthy plants, water and fertilize withered branches, move plants, and till the earth even in areas where nothing has been planted. Do you really need to take all this trouble?"

The Chan Master gardener explained, "Caring for plants is like teaching students or raising children. First, one must trim off areas such as unruly vines and foliage. Though vibrant, they grow without control. Only after such pruning are plants able to develop properly. This is similar to tempering the hot-headedness and eliminating the bad habits of the young, guiding them back to the right path.

Secondly, the purpose behind uprooting plants and repotting them is to remove them from barren soil and bringing them to fertile ground. This is just like removing the young from unhealthy environments and placing them into contact with kind mentors and beneficial friends for seeking higher learning.

Thirdly, one must water the withering branches. Though they seem dead on the outside, they contain in-finite potential for life within. Do not assume that your unruly children are hopeless and give up on them. People's nature is basically benevolent. Cherish and protect them, give them proper care, and they will eventually be reborn.

Fourthly, we loosen up soil so that seeds have room to sprout. This is like how when we give a hand to students who are eager to learn but lack the means to study by providing them with the opportunity to excel, grow, and achieve prosperity!"

The devotee heard this and said to the Chan Master gardener, "Thank you for teaching me the way of nurturing."

There is no life in this world that cannot be saved, no human potential beyond nurturing. At the entrance of temples there is often a statue of a laughing Maitreya Buddha. He represents reformation through compassion. Behind Maitreya Buddha is the temple's guardian deity General Skanda, holding a māra-subjugating vajra. He signifies that if compassion fails, you can be subdued with discipline. If parents and teachers are prepared to educate the next generation together through both love and discipline, those young people are sure to be successful individuals.

Waterwheel Principle

One day, during Chan Master Wuxiang's travels, he became thirsty and began to look for water. He saw a youth close by turning a waterwheel in a pond. Chan Master Wuxiang approached the youth and asked him for a bowl of water. Full of admiration, the youth said, "Chan Master! If one day I see through the red dust of *saṃsāra*, I will become a monk who seeks the Way like you. However, after I become a monk, I do not intend to wander about without a roof over my head. I will find a reclusive place where I can devote myself to meditation and avoid the hardships of living in the rough."

Chan Master Wuxiang replied, "Oh! Well then, when will you see through the red dust?"

The youth replied, "No one here knows the waterwheel as well as I. The whole village relies on it for water. If I could find someone to take my place in looking after the waterwheel, I would no longer be tied down by this responsibility. Then I could become a monk."

Chan Master Wuxiang replied, "Since you know the waterwheel so well, tell me, what happens if the waterwheel is completely submerged in, or completely removed from the water?"

The youth responded, "The waterwheel depends upon the bottom half being below water, pushing the top in the opposite direction of the current to create a continuous cyclical motion. If the bottom carts were totally submerged in water, not only does it cease to function, the waterwheel may be carried away by the river. Similarly, if the waterwheel is completely removed from the water, it would no longer bring water up."

Chan Master Wuxiang replied, "The relationship between the waterwheel and water is analogous to the relationship between humanity and the world. If people immerse themselves fully into the stream of worldliness, they will be swept away by the currents of the five desires and the red dust. If one completely cuts themselves off from mundane concerns, becomes pretentious and lofty, and by not interacting with the world, their life will have no grounding, incapable of developing or making progress. One who cultivates the Way should act with propriety. They must neither be a detached observer nor an active participant. For monastics, merely seeing through the red dust of worldliness is insufficient. One must also make the great vow to liberate all sentient beings. One combines both leaving and entering the mundane world, which is the correct attitude of monastics dealing with people and situations in their study of the Way."

Overjoyed, the youth said, "Chan Master, your words have opened my eyes. You truly are my guide to the Dharma."

If one is too attached to the five desires and sense objects of mundane life, then one will be burned by their fiery craving. If one single-mindedly attempts to escape from mundane affairs, then one will sink into frigid life-lessness. In life, it is best to let go when the time to let go arises and to pick up when the time for engagement arises. Like the waterwheel, we should try to follow the Middle Way. It is said that high-minded ideals require down-to-earth actions. There is much truth to these words.

A Pile of Firewood

One time, Chan Master Shítóu Xīqiān from Húnán, asked a student monk who had just recently arrived for his studies, "Where are you from?"

The student monk respectfully replied, "I am from Jiāngxī."

Chan Master Shítóu continued by asking, "Oh! Well, if you're from Jiāngxī, you must have seen Chan Master Mǎzǔ Dàoyī, right?"

The student monk answered, "Yes, I've seen him."

Chan Master Shítóu casually pointed to a pile of firewood on the ground next to him, and then asked the student monk, "Was Chan Master Mǎzǔ Dàoyī like this pile of firewood?" The student monk did not know what to say.

Since he could not connect with what Chan Master Shitou was teaching, he returned to Jiāngxī to see Chan Master Mǎzǔ Dàoyī, and he recounted the entire verbal exchange between he and Chan Master Shítóu. After listening to his story, Chan Master Mǎzǔ smiled indifferently. He asked the student monk, "How heavy did that pile of firewood look?"

The student monk responded, "I didn't get a careful measurement."

Chan Master Mǎzǔ said, "You're really quite strong."

Puzzled, the student monk asked, "Why do you say that?"

Chan Master Mǎzǔ replied, "You carried that pile of firewood all the way from Nanyue to here. How could that not be considered a feat of strength?"

During the Tang dynasty, young student monks would go either to study under Chan Master Mǎzǔ in Jiāngxī or Chan Master Shítóu in Húnán. People would travel from Jiāngxī to Húnán and from Húnán to Jiāngxī. That is where the saying "wandering back and forth from between Jiāng and Hú" originated. In the past, "wandering back and forth from between Jiāng and Hú" was used to mean that one was busy in his or her studies. Now "wandering back and forth from between Jiāng and Hú" has evolved to suggest that a person makes a living as a wandering artist.

This particular student monk went back and forth between Húnán to Jiāngxī, and tried to sow discord between the two masters. They not only remained unprovoked but also served him with a sober reminder of his own foolishness. These days, some Buddhist practitioners also go from temple to temple, carrying piles of firewood upon their backs. They are completely oblivious to the burden they are carrying.

Where is the Great Bodhisattva?

Chan Master Wúdé had strong resolve in spreading the Dharma and benefitting beings. Typically, all it took was a single request for teachings and he would happily speak with no signs of tiring. Aside from this, he constantly applied himself in the promotion of activities related to Buddhist culture, education, and philanthropy. Whenever any need arose within the community, he would immediately strive to assist them in any way he was able. Day after day, many years came to pass in this manner, and Chan Master Wúdé slowly gathered the support of many disciples and the unanimous praise of the Buddhist community.

One day, Chan Master Wúdé's chief disciple overheard a monk from a neighboring temple compliment his master, "Speak about Master Wúdé? What a truly commendable master! Not only is he compassionate to everyone, he also strives on the path while spreading the Dharma, benefiting beings, and dedicating himself to Buddhism. Chan Master Wúdé truly is a great bodhisattva!"

When the disciple heard these words of praise about his master he was overjoyed. When he returned to the monastery, he immediately hurried over to his master. Beaming with joy, he reported to Chan Master Wúdé that a monk from a neighboring monastery saw Chan Master Wúdé and considered him a great bodhisattva.

Who would have known that Chan Master Wúdé would suddenly ask his disciple, "Where is the great bodhisattva? Go on and tell me!"

Chan Master Wúdé's disciple spent every day with his master who behaved as a bodhisattva in the human realm and yet he had failed to notice the ways in which his master was different from other people. Consequently, when his master suddenly asked him this question, he found himself dumbstruck and unable to answer.

Regarding people in their current lives, if we were to separate them into three grades: upper grade, medium grade, and lower grade, then people in the upper grade would be those who do their best to benefit humanity no matter what it is they find themselves doing. They involve themselves in endeavors which serve the common good. As for the medium grade, their lives are rather ordinary yet do things for others but expect that others do things for them as well. Then there are those who only wish to take, these are the lower grade. There are even some who would not so much as lift a finger to help others around them, and they do not even fit into the lower grade.

With regards to the upper and medium grades, these individuals receive praise and admiration in much the same manner that Chan Master Wúdé did for the way that he continually cared for others. This is something which should be quite natural. If you have never done anything which led to others singing your praises, that is just fine too. To take the responsibility as a bodhisattva, one must steady oneself for studying, self-improvement, and progress upon the path. This in and of itself is praiseworthy. Moreover, in life it is not necessary to wait for the praise of others. If instead one takes the initiative to compliment others, then that too is of great value because offering praise is also emphatic joy and merit.

What is a Bodhisattva?

During the Tang dynasty, there was a young Chan monk who had heard of the renowned Chan Master Chángshā Jìngcén and decided to pay him a visit.

The first question he asked Chan Master Jìngcén was "Who is Mañjuśrī?"

Chan Master Jìngcén replied, "You are."

Next, the young monk asked another question, "Who is Samantabhadra?"

Chan Master Jìngcén again replied, "You are."

The young monk asked again, "Who is Avalokitêśvara?"

Chan Master Jìngcén replied yet again, "You are."

Confused, the monk asked, "Then who is Kṣitigarbha?"

Chan Master Jìngcén still answered, "You are."

No matter what this young monk asked him, Chan Master Jìngcén replied with two words: "You are."

The young monk finally became really suspicious and asked, "Chan Master, I am unable to comprehend your words."

Chan Master Jìngcén responded, "Why is it that you are unable to comprehend such a simple question?"

The young monk then remarked, "Mañjuśrī, Samantabhadra, Avalokitêśvara, and Kṣitigarbha had all cultivated throughout hundreds of thousands of *kalpas*. I am just an ordinary monk. How could I be Mañjuśrī, Samantabhadra, Avalokitêśvara, and Kṣitigarbha? How could I dare compare myself with them?"

Chan Master Jǐngcén let out a heartfelt laugh and said, "Avalokitêśvara Bodhisattva is compassionate; do you have compassion?"

The young monk answered, "A little."

Chan Master Jǐngcén continued, "Kṣitigarbha Bodhisattva had the strength of vows. You renounced to become a monk, you have the strength of vows, don't you?"

The monk answered, "I have some."

Chan Master Jǐngcén asked another question: "Mañjuśrī was complete with wisdom. Do you have wisdom?"

The monk answered, "I suppose I have some."

Lastly, Chan Master Jǐngcén asked, "Have you practiced asceticism?"

The young monk nodded his head and then with great certainty he replied, "Yes, I have!"

Chan Master Jǐngcén finally responded, "There it is! When you received ordination, didn't you all acknowledge before your preceptors that you were a bodhisattva? Why are you now reluctant to shoulder that responsibility?" With these words the young monk finally awakened to their meaning.

After Mahāyāna Buddhism spread to China, the so called "Four Great Mountains" were recognized as sacred sites over time. They are namely, Mañjuśrī Bodhisattva at Mount Wǔtái, Shānxī province; Avalokitêśvara Bodhisattva at Mount Pǔtuó, Zhèjiāng province; Kṣitigarbha Bodhisattva at Mount Jiǔhuá, Ānhuī province; and Samantabhadra Bodhisattva at Mount Éméi, Sìchuān province. These four great bodhisattvas are the emblem of Chinese Mahāyāna Buddhism, the primary spirit of which is "compassion, wisdom, vow, and practice."

When monks are ordained, they all receive the bodhisattva precepts. They must first vow to become bodhisattvas and receive the bodhisattva precepts. When Śākyamuni Buddha attained enlightenment, he proclaimed that all sentient beings have the wisdom and virtue of the Tathāgata. All people are buddhas. It is just that due to their delusional attachments, they are unable to realize enlightenment. If they are able to recognize that "I am a buddha;" why wouldn't they be able to accept that they are bodhisattvas?

Venerable Master Tàixū once said, "I'm not a bhikṣu and not yet a buddha, please just call me a bodhisattva." We can be certain that we are bodhisattvas since we practice the bodhisattva path, how could this not be the case?

What is the Practice of Avalokiteśvara?

Mount Lú's Chan Master Guīzōng Zhìcháng was a native of Húběi. He was a Dharma heir of Chan Master Mǎzǔ Dàoyī. Chan Master Zhìcháng was not inclined to use pretentious language in conveying principles, instead he utilized functional Chan that was applicable to daily life. This approach was both lively and inspiring.

One day, Chan Master Zhìcháng was teaching the entire assembly: "Today I will speak with you all regarding the state of Chan. Would everyone please move in closer?"

The audience heard this and moved closer to the Chan master.

Chan Master Zhìcháng stood silently for a moment before remarking, "The *Universal Gate Chapter* of the *Lotus Sūtra* contains the following verse: '"You listen now to the practice of Avalokiteśvara, who responds well to every region.' Do each of you understand the meaning of this verse?"

The assembly just looked back and forth at one another. None of them knew what Chan Master Zhìcháng had in store for them. From within the crowd, one monk called out, "Chan Master, could you please tell us 'the practice of Avalokiteśvara'?" How should we go about 'responding well in every region?'"

Chan Master Zhìcháng replied, "Go, go, go!"

When he heard this, the monk answered, "Thank you, Chan Master. We will go 'respond well in every region.'" After he finished speaking, he led the assembly to disperse. Chan Master Zhìcháng laughed uproariously and remarked, "You get it! You get it!" He then returned to his quarters.

The Universal Gate Chapter *contains many gathas which praise Avalokitêśvara Bodhisattva's practice and "responds well in every region." This verse describes how Avalokitêśvara Bodhisattva travels to every land to liberate and enlighten sentient beings, wandering like a cloud. The term "wandering" indicates that the Bodhisattva does not feel burdened by this. Avalokitêśvara enjoys great freedom in traveling, saving beings as their conditions permit. It is different from the excessive attempts from some individuals bent on "making a difference." Because Avalokitêśvara practices compassion, virtue, and wisdom, the Bodhisattva is able to wander, employing skillful means while adapting to accommodate all locations, times, and people.*

What is the "practice of Avalokitêśvara?" It means to freely wander the lands, liberating sentient beings. However, Chan Master Zhìcháng did not directly explain this. Instead he answered, "Go, go, go!" Understanding this, the monk replied, "We will respond well in every region." When the master saw how quickly everyone comprehended the teaching, he could not help but burst out laughing, remarking, "You get it! You get it!"

Not a Buddha is a True Buddha

During the Tang dynasty the young Chan Master Dòng-shān Liángjià went to Jīngzhào (present day Xī'ān in Shǎnxī province) to study with Monk Xìng Píng, one of the Dharma heirs of Chan Master Mǎzǔ Dàoyī.

When Chan Master Dòngshān Liángjià first laid eyes on Monk Xìng Píng, he was about to bow before him, but he did not expect Monk Xìng Píng to preemptively shout, "There is no need to bow before this old fellow."

Hearing this, Chan Master Dòngshān Liángjià quickly remarked, "Today I came not to pay homage to some old fellow, but to a buddha" and he continued by further remarking, "Devotees come to pay reverence to buddhas, and buddhas have never refused them."

Monk Xìng Píng replied, "That is why I told you that I am not a buddha."

Chan Master Dòngshān Liángjià smiled and answered, "Not a buddha is a true buddha!"

At this point, Monk Xìng Píng finally responded by saying, "Fine, so are you, so are you!" With that, he returned a bow to Chan Master Dòngshān Liángjià. In that way the two connected their minds and became friends in Chan.

Buddhism has many customs. When it comes to bowing before a buddha, one usually bows three times and it would not be appropriate to only bow once. Why is that? It is done that way because when it is called out, "bow, offering three prostrations," of course the icons of the Buddha will not say anything back, and therefore we bow three times, but bowing to a person is quite different. One only bows one time, and if the intention to prostrate before a person is announced, since said person is alive, he or she can interject by saying, "Just bow once please." Consequently, if someone ever tells you to offer three prostrations to a living person, this is not actually in keeping with Buddhist etiquette.

We seek the Dharma with reverence. One should venerate one's elders, and elders should accept veneration with propriety. Chan Master Dòngshān Liángjià wanted to pay his respects to Monk Xìng Píng, but since Monk Xìng Píng recused himself with "this old fellow is not a buddha," he refused Chan Master Dòngshān Liángjià's veneration. After a short dispute, the two honored each other as equals and paid each other mutual veneration. Both were true buddhas, understanding the Way.

The Buddha's Worries

Once, a devotee asked Chan Master Zhàozhōu Cóng-shěn, "Does the Buddha have any worries?"

Chan Master Zhàozhōu answered, "Yes!"

"The Buddha is the founder of our religion, a liberated being. How could he have any worries?"

"The Buddha has worries because you have not yet attained enlightenment." Chan Master Zhàozhōu answered.

"Well, if I cultivate until I attain liberation, would the Buddha have any worries?"

Chan Master Zhàozhōu answered, "Yes!"

The devotee asked again, "But given that I attained liberation, why would the Buddha still have worries?"

"Because there are other sentient beings!"

"Sentient beings are countless and limitless. There is no way to liberate every last one of them. As such, the Buddha will have worries forever. How can one possibly transcend that?" The devotee asked.

"He already achieved transcendence. The Buddha doesn't have any worries anymore!"

"You're saying that the Buddha doesn't have any worries anymore, but there are still sentient being who have yet to be liberated. How is it that the Buddha doesn't have worries?"

"The sentient beings within the Buddha's self-nature have already been liberated."

Another devotee asked Chan Master Zhàozhōu, "Where will a great practitioner such as yourself be after you pass away?"

"To be honest, I will be in hell!" Chan Master Zhàozhōu replied.

"Chan Master, how could someone with such high level of cultivation end up in hell?" The disciple asked, confused.

"If I didn't go to hell, who would rescue you?"

From this we can see that the worries of ordinary humans and sentient beings arises from ignorance and deluded thoughts. The worries of buddhas arise out of compassion. To say that the Buddha has no worries can be said on the basis of wisdom. Worries for the Buddha or Chan Master Zhàozhōu's descent to hell can be said on the basis of compassion and pity for the misery experienced by sentient beings who are suffering from worries. The worries of bodhisattvas is that which comes from compassion. The worries of ordinary humans comes from worries itself; it also comes from karmic hindrances.

There is no need to fear worries. "Do not fear arising thoughts; just fear that awareness comes late!" If you have awareness then you have compassion and wisdom, why fear worries?

Characteristic of the Enlightened

In the Japanese Rinzai School there was a monk known as Zen Master Hakuin Ekaku. He was a native of Shizuoka Prefecture and became a monk at Shōin Temple at fifteen. He received the Dharma from Zen Master Shōju Rōjin in Iiyama, Shinano (Nagano Prefecture).

Zen Master Hakuin did not seek fame and fortune while he traveled throughout Japan spreading the Dharma and instructing students. He liberated and taught sentient beings according to the situation and circumstances. Through his efforts, he revitalized the declining Rinzai School.

One of Zen Master Hakuin's many lay disciples was Madam Masako. She already had achieved some Zen and her understanding was met with the approval of the Zen Master.

One time, Madam Masako's beloved daughter passed away from illness and Zen Master Hakuin with his disciples came to visit her. When they arrived at the gates of her home, they saw that she was behaving just as an ordinary person would, weeping in anguish at the daughter she lost. A handful of lay Buddhists surrounding her could not help but frown as they advised her, "Hold back your tears! You are an enlightened person, and should understand the principle of impermanence. How come you are so sad?" Madam Masako did not cease her crying in response to their pleas, instead, she cried all the harder.

When they saw that their pleas were not being heeded, helplessly, their eyes moved towards Zen Master Hakuin awaiting his intervention, and he said nothing. He just compassionately watched over Madam Masako. A short time passed before Zen Master Hakuin finally turned back toward the crowd. He addressed them with a question, "What do you think enlightened people are like?" Zen Master Hakuin continued speaking, "Is it really the case that enlightened people lack real emotions? In truth, that is not the case. When a person experiences the awakening of the Dharma, and still will not lose his or her human nature and be able to transcend it; that is a true practitioner of the Way. I would say, someone who is able to still cry loudly can be said to be truly enlightened to the Way."

Over 2,500 years ago, the Buddha announced that he was about to enter Parinirvāṇa. His disciples felt like their world had been turned upside down, and neither sun nor moon could brighten the dark skies of their sorrow. The Honorable Ānanda, who served as the Buddha's attendant likewise shed sad tears. When the Buddha had reached Parinirvāṇa between two sala trees, the devas lamented, his disciples wept, and loud wails echoed through the air. Even the Honorable Mahākāśyapa, who was returning from afar began crying ceaselessly. Although they fully comprehended the Dharma and were sages who had awakened to the truth, they still possessed human emotions. Therefore, Zen Master Hakuin offered Madam Masako understanding and loving-kindness. This should not be difficult to understand. It is known as common sense!

A Flash of Anger from
the Son of Heaven

Chan Master Tiāntóng Dàomín received the Dharma from Chan Master Mìyún Yuánwù. After Chan Master Yuánwù passed away, Chan Master Tiāntóng Dàomín inherited his Dharma seat and became the abbot of Níngbō Tiāntóng Temple. At that time, Emperor Shùnzhì of the Qing dynasty deeply respected and appreciated Chan Master Tiāntóng Dàomín's Chan style. He even bestowed the honorific title "Chan Master Hóngjué (Great Enlightenment)" on him.

Chan Master Tiāntóng Dàomín heard that Emperor Shùnzhì's disposition is stern and reclusive such that even his ministers had great difficulty approaching him. All it took was any matter not to his liking and he would lash out at the attendants by his side. One time, Emperor Shùnzhì requested the Chan Master's guidance. Chan Master Dàomín said:

"Those who learn Chan and study the Way must understand clearly in his mind regarding both positive and negative states. They should not give in to reckless abandon nor should they be unsteady in their joy or anger. The great scholar Fù of the Southern dynasty once said, 'The nature of the mind is empty and serene; the form of greed and anger is tangible.' This is also what was meant by Samantabhadra Bodhisattva when he said, 'I have yet to see any phenomenon that is a more serious fault than anger.'

Your highness, the saying 'one thought of anger opens up a million gates of obstacles' is the precise explanation of this same truth."

Emperor Shùnzhì deeply contemplated Chan Master Dàomín's words. After much thought, he replied, "Every time that I face situations, I lack the awareness to reflect upon my emotions. Once the state has passed, it evaporates like water, no longer lingering in my mind."

Chan Master Dàomín replied, "Your highness's mind is like the empty space and the luminous moon, devoid of discrimination. However, your highness's emotions of joy and anger are a great deal different from that of ordinary people."

"What do you mean by that?" Emperor Shùnzhì asked in amazement.

Chan Master Dàomín spoke again saying, "There is a saying, 'Just a flash of anger from the son of heaven, and corpses lie upon the ground for thousands of miles.' Although these emotions may not linger upon your highness's mind, waiting to address them until after they have passed will be too late to avoid their consequences!"

Emperor Shùnzhì considered this. Finally, he nodded and said, "I understand."

Later, the Emperor's attendant, Lǐ Guózhù, had a chance encounter with Chan Master Tiāntóng Dàomín. Cheerfully, he proclaimed, "Chan Master, Chan Master! The Emperor has not only ceased ordering people beaten, now he rarely even scolds others!"

Everyone should set their own personal standards. Some people hold themselves to the letter of the law, follow certain ethical codes, and uphold the morality laid down by their religious faiths. On the path of life there should always be rules and standards.

The emperors and kings of the past wanted their subjects to be law-abiding and follow the Way, but they themselves would do whatever they pleased. Consequently, their political system of autocracy was culpable to those who suffered lives of misfortune and haunted by those who died unjust deaths. Since Chan Master Tiāntóng Dàomín did not have many Chan methods to enlighten Emperor Shùnzhì, he simply offered many examples in his explanations. His emotions as an individual affected the happiness and unhappiness of all his subjects. Emperor Shùnzhì was already considered a sensible ruler, but after receiving Chan Master Tiāntóng Dàomín's recommendations, he improved his character. He ceased complaining about those around him. He turned his indignant dislike of them into praise for them, and he turned his resentment into happiness. Such is the efficacy of the Dharma.

Offerings from a Deva

Venerable Master Dàoxuān was known as the Master of Nánshān *Vinaya* School, renowned for the propagation of the *vinaya* teachings. He strictly upheld the precepts and *vinaya* his entire life, had but one meal a day and his practice even moved a *deva* to offer him a meal daily.

A contemporary of *Vinaya* Master Dàoxuān during the Tang dynasty, Venerable Master Kuījī who was known as the "Three Carriage Monk," hailed from a prominent family and a foremost disciple of Venerable Master Xuánzàng. At the time, Venerable Master Xuánzàng was able to see with his wisdom eye that Kuījī had deep wholesome roots and wanted to bring him into the gates of Buddhism to be a monk. Kuījī came up with three conditions under which he would become a monk: "A carriage full of beautiful women, a carriage full of alcohol, and a carriage full of books." Venerable Master Xuánzàng agreed and Kuījī came under the Venerable Master to study Buddhist *sutras* and treatises.

One day, Venerable Kuījī experienced a sudden enlightenment: "Dharma is filled with Chan bliss and Dharma joy which can be experienced all the time. Why be dragged down by mundane pleasures?" So he set aside his three carriages and devoted himself to translate *sutras* and speak on treatises, taking the propagation of the Mind-Only teachings his life's mission.

Vinaya Master Dàoxuān respected Venerable Master Kuījī's profound knowledge and skillful eloquence, but he was deeply against the "three carriages" Kuījī once possessed.

So it was that Venerable Master Kuījī was passing through Mount Zhōngnán and decided to visit Venerable Master Dàoxuān. Venerable Master Dàoxuān wished to utilize the sight of the celestial being offering a meal as an opportunity to inspire Venerable Master Kuījī to practice more diligently. The two met and conversed quite well with one another. Before they knew it, they had spent the entire midday period with one another, however the *deva* had been running late and he did not come by to make his offering. It was only after Venerable Master Kuījī got up and left that the *deva* finally came to make an offering.

Venerable Master Dàoxuān was confused and asked the celestial being, "Why were you late today with the offering?"

The celestial being replied, "I couldn't help it. There was a great Mahāyāna bodhisattva here. Hundreds of thousands of Dharma guardians and protectors surrounded him. There was no way I could have gotten through to be here!"

Upon hearing this, Venerable Master Dàoxuān was shocked and felt deeply ashamed. From then, Venerable Master Dàoxuān had great sincerity and respect for Venerable Master Kuījī and never dared to give rise to any arrogance towards him again.

Venerable Master Kuījī upheld precepts of the mind as his discreet practice. Whether walking, standing, sitting, or lying down he actualized the Dharma, a Mahayana bodhisattva who was not attached to the appearance of cultivation. Vinaya Master Dàoxuān adhered to the precepts strictly, however, this led to him becoming arrogant. A prideful mind runs contrary to the purity of one's original mind. Vinaya Master Dàoxuān wished to use the deva offering him his meals as a means of shaming Venerable Master Kuījī into stricter practice. He never imagined that Venerable Master Kuījī was a discreet practitioner of the bodhisattva path who ultimately offered Vinaya Master Dàoxuān a lesson.

Great and Small Are No Different

Lǐ Bó was young, successful, high-spirited, and during the Tang dynasty, he was head of Jiāngzhōu prefecture. One time, he went to request instruction from Chan Master Guīzōng Zhìcháng. Lǐ Bó believed that the oft-heard phrase in Buddhism, "*Mount Sumeru* stores a mustard seed; a mustard seed holds Mount Sumeru" was not only peculiar and profound, but also rather illogical. He felt this way because while it made sense that *Mount Sumeru* could store a mustard seed, how could a tiny mustard seed somehow hold Mount Sumeru? That must be a lie, right?

Chan Master Guīzōng heard these questions and let out a laugh. He asked a question right back to Lǐ Bó; "People have said that you 'read ten thousand scrolls of books thoroughly, and your writing is divinely empowered.' Is that possible?"

"Well of course, of course! I've not only read ten thousand scrolls of books thoroughly, I've read over ten thousand scrolls!" Lǐ Bó said with an air of elation.

Chan Master Guīzōng continued his questioning: "Well, in that case, could I please ask, where then are those ten thousand scrolls of books that you have read?"

Lǐ Bó pointed towards his head and answered, "I've read the ten thousands scrolls of books into my brain."

The Chan Master remarked, "That's strange. It looks to me that your brain is no bigger than a pineapple or about the size of a coconut. How could it contain ten thousand scrolls of books? Unless of course you're lying to me."

After Lǐ Bó heard this, there was a thundering in his mind and in that moment he gained a deep degree of understanding.

In the Dharma, sometimes explanations are based on phenomena and other times explanations are based on principles. Just as the universe has myriad phenomena, phenomena also contains myriad principles. Within those principles, there is also phenomena. Phenomena cannot abandon principles and principles cannot be devoid of phenomena. Phenomena and principles require to be harmonized. "Mount Sumeru storing a mustard seed" is a phenomena. "A mustard seed holding Mount Sumeru" is a principle. If we can understand phenomena and principles without any hindrance, then we will succeed in integrating the universe's original essence with phenomenal appearance, and we will succeed in integrating self and other. Original essence and phenomenal appearance, self and other... these are all equanimous. There is no right or wrong between them. Is this not the state of freeness and ease?

The Great Chiliocosm is a Chan Bed

Chan Master Wúxué Zǔyuán was a native of Míngzhōu Yínxiàn (present day Zhèjiāng) during the southern Song dynasty. He served as the Head Monk of Tiāntóng Temple. Later in his years, he received an invitation from the eighth Shikken (regent of a shogun), Hōjō Tokimune, and headed east to Japan to expound Chan teachings; it was there that he became the founder of Engaku Temple.

One day, a devotee who was serving as an administrative official paid Chan Master Zǔyuán a visit and asked him, "Chan Master, thank you for your guidance in the method of seated meditation yesterday. However, your disciple cannot help it, but has been busy with official duties and cannot practice in quiet, serene environments. Chan Master, it is my hope that you can compassionately guide us through a more convenient method."

Chan Master Zǔyuán replied, "Practice is not a matter of being in a quiet or noisy place. At the same time though, one does not depart from a quiet or noisy place."

The devotee heard this and thought it was rather odd. He asked again, "I have often heard that in order to enter the Way, one needs to practice seated meditation in a meditation hall. However, you have said that meditation is not about leaving quiet or noisy places. Ultimately then, where should we practice?"

Chan Master Zǔyuán asked him, "When you are busy do you ever forget about being hungry?"

The devotee responded, "No."

The Chan Master continued, "Do you forget to go to the bathroom?"

The devotee again answered, "No."

The Chan Master asked once more, "So when you eat or go to the bathroom, do you have to think about those needs in order to remember them or do you just eat and go to the bathroom when those needs arise?"

The devotee responded, "I don't need to think about those sorts of things. When I need to take care of them I just go and do it."

Chan Master Zǔyuán nodded his head and remarked, "That's exactly right. The entire *chiliocosm* is but a Chan bed!"

The devotee suddenly comprehended the master's teaching and nodded his head joyfully.

Some people seek out areas of quietude deep within mountains. However, even upon reaching those tranquil areas deep in the mountains, one's mind may still fail to settle down as one continues to think about the red dust of secular life. One may be in the mountain forest, but the mind is still in the red dust, so that is not the answer. One may like cultivating in noisy and lively areas, spending every day following the red dust in the winds of change, so the mind cannot be calmed. Whether it is movement or stillness, one's mind is never calm.

A Chan practitioner lived in a meditation hall for two years. One day, he suddenly re-entered society and standing at a four-way intersection he proclaimed loudly, "How can a Chan practitioner be taken as worthy if he cannot hold up the sky and traverse the earth? When the mind does not embrace the multitude of sentient beings, how can he be taken worthy of practicing Chan and reciting the Buddha's name?" The chiliocosm is but a Chan bed! So long as one has a calm mind, is there anywhere that cannot be taken as the place for practice?

The Body Which Does Not Fall Ill

After studying under Chan masters such as Nánquán Pǔyuàn, Wéishān Língyòu, and Yúnyán Tánchéng, Chan Master Dòngshān Liángjià gazed upon his reflection in the water and gained profound understanding. Chan Master Dòngshān had traveled to the provinces of Jiāngxī, Ānhuī, Húběi, and Húnán before finally settling in Pǔlì Monastery on Mount Dòng in Jiāngxī province for ten years. Within Pǔlì Monastery, his Dharma assembly bloomed, and he attracted countless students. Among his students, Chan Master Yúnjū Dàoyīng and Chan Master Cáoshān Běnjì became the most well-known and distinguished.

When Chan Master Dòngshān was near life's end at age sixty-three, Chan Master Cáoshān asked him, "Master, your body has fallen ill, but is there a body that is not subject to illness?"

Chan Master Dòngshān answered in the affirmative, "There is!"

Chan Master Cáoshān asked further, "Can this body which is not subject to illness be seen?"

Chan Master Dòngshān laughed, "Yes, I am looking at it."

Confused, Chan Master Cáoshān asked, "How is it that you can see it, Master?"

Chan Master Dòngshān replied, "When I see it, I do not see illness!"

Shortly after that exchange, Chan Master Dòngshān felt his body was not well. He got up to bathe, put on his *kāṣāya* (monastic robes), sounded the temple bell, bid farewell to the monastic community, and peaceful sat in meditation until he passed away.

The student monks began to weep. Chan Master Dòngshān suddenly opened his eyes and yelled, "Minds of monastics don't rely on any matter; that is true cultivation. What are you all grieving about?" Chan Master Dòngshān ordered someone to go prepare a "feast for the ignorant."

Knowing that Chan Master Dòngshān would pass away after the meal, the student monks delayed the feast for seven days. After he ate the meal, Chan Master Dòngshān addressed them, "Always remember that when a person passes on, there should be no unseemly mourning. From now on, Cáoshān will be your teacher!"

The physical body is subject to illness. This is something which is easily seen and understood. The Dharmakāya (Dharma Body) is not subject to illness. This cannot be seen and cannot be understood. That is why Chan Master Dòngshān said to Chan Master Cáoshān "I cannot see illness!" The physical body will experience birth, ageing, sickness, and death, but the essential nature of Dharmakāya does not have birth, ageing, sickness, or death. The physical body and fleshly form cannot be separated from the essential nature of Dharmakāya. Nor can the essential nature of Dharmakāya be separated from the physical body. However, how is it that one can realize the essential nature of Dharmakāya through the physical body and fleshly form? Contemplate!

Not in Disharmony

Chan Master Qīngliáng Xiūfù of Qingliang Temple in Jiangsu was a native of Běihǎi, (present day Wéifāng in Shāndōng province). He became a monk early in his youth, and at age nineteen he was fully ordained. After receiving ordination, he traveled far and wide seeking renowned masters to learn Chan and practice the teaching. He awakened to the Way at Kṣitigarbha Temple under the tutelage of Chan Master Luóhàn Guìchēn, and received the essence of his Dharma.

Although Chan Master Xiūfù had studied the Dharma for many years, he was still unable to understand its essence thoroughly, resulting in serious illness to the point where he was taken to the Nirvāṇa Hall to recover.

One day, Chan Master Guìchēn went to visit him. Concerned, Guìchēn asked, "Has your illness gotten any better?"

Chan Master Xiūfù answered sadly, "This student is quite dull, and I think my karmic causes and conditions must be out of harmony with yours. I still cannot understand the essence of the Dharma and cannot connect."

Chan Master Guìchēn pointed to a nearby lantern and asked, "Do you see this?"

Chan Master Xiūfù nodded, "Yes, I see it."

Chan Master Guìchēn gave him a compassionate look and said, "You see, this is it. You and I are not in disharmony!"

When these words reached Chan Master Xiūfù's ears, his mind lit up like a lamp and his illness was half-gone.

Several days later, Chan Master Guìchēn was feeling unwell. Chan Master Xiūfù stayed by his side to care for him. Chan Master Guìchēn's other disciple, Chan Master Lóngjì Shàoxiū came to visit his master.

Chan Master Shàoxiū first offered his greeting and then stated, "Throughout hundreds of *kalpas* and thousands of lives, your disciple always had causes and conditions which were out of harmony with yours. Today I have come here, how should we go about connecting in harmony?"

Chan Master Guìchēn heard this and again pointed to the lantern asking, "Do you see this lantern?"

Chan Master Shàoxiū replied, "Yes, I see it."

Chan Master Guìchēn replied, "You see? This is it. We are not in disharmony!"

From beside them, Chan Master Xiūfù interjected, "We only see the lantern, but not the candle!"

Chan Master Guìchēn answered, "The candle is lit inside your mind. You are not looking inwards. What are you looking for outside?"

Upon hearing this, both Xiūfù and Shàoxiū simultaneously attained enlightenment.

In this world, we can use our eyes to see myriad phenomena and objects. All those things and objects have their own causes and conditions. To "see" their causes and conditions, we must use our mind. If we are looking here, we are unable to see what is there. If we are looking near, we cannot see far. Only seeing appearances, we do not see their essence. If we look outward, we cannot see what is within, consequently there is ignorance and enlightenment; so being able to see the inner candle from the outward appearance of the lantern is the true practice of Chan.

My Body is Seventeen

The lineage of Chan Buddhism began with the Buddha's transmission of the Dharma to the Honorable Mahākāśyapa. The second transmission was to the Honorable Ānanda, the third was to the Honorable Śāṇakavāsa, and the fourth was to the Honorable Upagupta.

The wanderings of the Third Patriarch Śāṇakavāsa brought him to the kingdom of Pāṭaliputra, where he came across Upagupta. Detecting extraordinary potential in the youth before him, Śāṇakavāsa decided to test him by asking, "Young man, how old are you?"

Upagupta replied, "I am seventeen."

Śāṇakavāsa using a Chan approach asked him, "Is it your body which is seventeen or is your original nature seventeen?"

Upagupta returned with the question, "Chan Master, I see that your hair is as white as snow. May I please ask, is it your hair or your mind that is white?"

Śāṇakavāsa smiled and answered, "Of course it is my hair, not my mind!"

Upagupta then said, "That's right! Naturally, it is my body which is seventeen, and not my original nature."

Śāṇakavāsa was pleased by this answer, and took Upagupta as his attendant. After three years Upagupta became a monk, received full ordination, and was entrusted with the lineage transmission. Śāṇakavāsa said to him:

"The unsurpassed lineage was first transmitted by the Buddha to Mahākāśyapa. It was passed down for generations until it reached me. Today I entrust the unsurpassed lineage to you; now it is up to you to protect and preserve it." Following those words he recited a transmission gāthā which imparted the Dharma to Upagupta, making him the Fourth Patriarch. The transmission gāthā was as follows:

"Not Dharma, not mind, no mind, no Dharma; when speaking of the mind's Dharma, it is Dharma and not the mind's Dharma."

In India, Chan was transmitted through twenty eight generations of patriarchs. Afterwards, the Twenty Eighth Patriarch, Bodhidarma (the first patriarch of the Eastern Lands), traveled east to China. Over the course of six successive transmissions, the lineage came to the Sixth Patriarch Huìnéng. Due to contention regarding *his robes and alms bowl, from that point onwards, the robe was no longer used as a symbol of Dharma transmission; the Dharma was transmitted from mind to mind.*

When Śāṇakavāsa first encountered the seventeen year old Upagupta, he tested him on whether it was his physical body or original nature that was seventeen. Upagupta cleverly turned this question back upon Śāṇakavāsa asking, "Is it your hair or your original nature which is white?" The Honorable Śāṇakavāsa answered saying, "Of course it is my hair which is white. How could a person's original nature be white?" Upagupta echoed this, saying, "Well of course I am also seventeen years in age, and it is certainly not my original nature which is seventeen."

This dialogue between an elder and a youth clearly explain that Buddha Nature is formless, non-abiding, non-increasing, and non-decreasing. Everyone has Buddha Nature and it is timeless and unchanging. Even after countless kalpas, it is as good as new. It exists in the past, present, and future, and permeates all space throughout the ten directions. How then, can we attribute it an age or label it with physical characteristics? Although there is youth and old age in the world of phenomena, the original nature cannot be differentiated as such.

Death and Returning to Life

One time when Chan Master Nánquán Pǔyuàn was sitting in meditation, he suddenly gave a loud roar. His attendant was startled, and quickly rushed over to Chan Master Nánquán's side and asked him, "Master, are you okay?"

Chan Master Nánquán replied, "You go check on the Nirvāṇa Hall. Did someone just pass away?" On the way, the attendant and superintendent of the Nirvāṇa Hall bumped into one another in the hallway, so they both went to report to Chan Master Nánquán that indeed a wandering Chan monk who had been staying at the temple had just passed away. Right after they finished reporting, the monk serving as temple greeter hurried into the room.

The greeter said to Chan Master Nánquán: "The Chan monk who died just now has come back to life."

Chan Master Nánquán asked, "How is he now?"

The greeter monk replied, "He asked to see you, Chan Master. However, that monk never cultivated merit or virtue and was unwilling to create wholesome affinities. Nobody is particularly willing to help him."

Chan Master Nánquán went to the Nirvāṇa Hall to visit the sick Chan monk. He asked the Chan monk, "Where did you go just now?"

The sick monk answered, "I went to the netherworld!"

Chan Master Nánquán further inquired, "What is it like in the netherworld?"

The sick monk answered, "I walked about a hundred

miles, and then my arms and legs hurt too much to move any further. What made it especially hard was that my throat was dry with thirst. Just then, someone called to me and invited me to enter a great pavilion. Since I was so tired, I really wanted to go in to rest, but as soon as I got to the entrance of the pavilion, an old monk shouted at me to stay put. I was so startled I fell on my back. It was because of this that I can now come see you, teacher."

Chan Master Nánquán remarked, "That was truly a splendid and magnificent pavilion! However, how could you have entered it without having accumulated merit and virtue? If you had not come across the old monk, I am afraid you would have found yourself suffering in hell."

From that day onward, that Chan monk diligently worked to accumulate merit and virtue. At seventy, he passed away peacefully while in seated meditation. He became known as "Nánquán's Practitioner of the Way."

From within his state of meditative concentration, Chan Master Nánquán could travel freely to the heavens and hells. His roar within meditative concentration was able to bring the dead back to life. People say that Chan masters often behave in ways which seem cold and contrary to human emotion. However, those like Chan Master Nánquán cared for their disciples so much that they were even willing to follow them into hell and give them another chance at life. How could this be described as being out of touch with human sentimentality?

Chan does not run completely contrary to human emotion. There are also aspects of it which follow emotional conventions. It even enables practitioners to gain a profound mastery over emotional intelligence.

To Use Daily Yet Not Know

During Later Tang dynasty of the Five Dynasties period, there was a Chan Master named Xuánshā Shībèi who hailed from Mǐn county in Fúzhōu. He was the Dharma heir of Chan Master Xuěfēng Yìcún. After he received full ordination, he practiced Bei asceticism. Due to his vigorous practice of seated meditation, people also called him the "Bei Ascetic." Later in life, Chan Master Shībèi was able to immerse himself in the Dharma through study of the *Śūraṃgama Sūtra.* He moved to Mount Xuánshā where, for over thirty years, he taught the Dharma in accordance to the capacity of the community. Over eight hundred people came to learn from him, they were from all walks of life who climbed the mountain to ask for instructions in the Dharma.

One day, a military officer with the family name "Wéi" came to visit Chan Master Xuánshā Shībèi who offered some fruit to Wéi. As they ate, Wéi asked Chan Master Xuánshā Shībèi, "What does 'to use daily yet not know' mean?"

Chan Master Xuánshā Shībèi picked up a piece of fruit inviting him, "Here, have another."

Without thinking, Wéi replied, "Okay." He took the fruit and began eating it.

After finishing that piece of fruit, Wéi still did not understand. He asked once more, "Chan Master, now can you tell me the meaning of 'to use daily yet not know?'"

Chan Master Xuánshā Shībèi gave him a serious look and said, "What you just did was precisely 'to use daily yet not know.'"

Cultivation requires people to pay attention to that which is ordinary and occurs daily. In truth, where is the Dharma to be found if not inside our daily life?

On a smaller scale, Dharma enables people to solve the problems of daily living; on a larger scale, Dharma enables people to resolve the matter of birth and death. Only after simple life problems are taken care of can one take care of the problem of birth and death. What we use on a daily basis within walking, standing, sitting, or resting; it is within meeting the needs of getting food and shelter for oneself.

This military officer asked Chan Master Xuánshā Shībèi what daily use of the Dharma was, and Chan Master Xuánshā Shībèi gave him a piece of fruit. The giver and receiver should both experience Dharma, but the officer was unable to understand. After eating the fruit, he still asked what "to use daily yet not know?" meant. Of course, the Chan master taught him; "don't you understand the Dharma of daily life that we just engaged in?"

Once, someone asked a Chan master how to practice Chan. The master replied, "When you eat, eat your fill. When you sleep, sleep well." People who do not understand think that the Chan master speaks too simplistically. Everyone eats and sleeps; how is that Chan? But for Chan practitioners, people eat without appreciating their meal, they toss and turn in their sleep and ruin their rest, so how could that be considered Chan? Achieving ease, Dharma joy in daily life, and with an appreciation of Chan bliss, that is the practice of Chan.

Call it Sweet Cakes

One day, a monk went to visit Chan Master Mùzhōu Dàomíng. Chan Master Mùzhōu Dàomíng asked him, "Which aspect of Buddhism do you usually study?"

The student monk had nothing to hide so he just honestly replied, "I've been reading teachings on Mind-Only."

Chan Master Mùzhōu Dàomíng asked further, "Well then, are you well-versed enough to discuss the Mind-Only Treatise?"

The monk meekly replied, "I wouldn't dare presume."

Chan Master Mùzhōu Dàomíng picked up a sweet cake from the table and pulled it apart into two pieces. He asked the monk, "The three realms are mind-only, and all myriad phenomena are consciousness-only. How would you explain this?"

The monk was speechless.

Chan Master Mùzhōu Dàomíng would not let up and preceded to ask, "This here is called a sweet cake, right? Or should it perhaps not be called a sweet cake?"

Upon hearing that question, the monk became even more nervous. Sweating profusely he answered, "It cannot be 'not called' a sweet cake."

Chan Master Mùzhōu eyed the monk and then gently called upon the novice monk who was waiting on him, "If I split a sweet cake into two pieces, what would you say?"

Without any hesitation, the novice replied, "Two pieces reside within a single mind."

The Chan Master asked further, "What would you call them?"

The novice monk replied, "Sweet cakes."

Chan Master Mùzhōu Dàomíng couldn't restrain himself from laughing uproariously and saying, "It seems that you can also speak on the Mind-Only Treatise."

The study of Mind-Only teachings and the study of Chan have different methods and orientations. Mind-Only emphasizes intellectual knowledge and analysis whereas Chan does not emphasize reasoning and analysis. Chan points directly to the original mind allowing one to glimpse self-nature and achieve Buddhahood. The sayings of Chan masters are humorous, their attitudes are amiable and they do not enjoy stoic methods of teaching. Sometimes they say one thing but mean another, other times they may hit you or curse at you, but actually they love and protect you. Mind-Only adherents speak persuasively and clearly to impart Mind-Only teachings. In Chan, it only takes a few words: "So what do you call it?" "Sweet cakes." Just like that, "The three realms are mind-only, and all myriad phenomena are consciousness-only" is expressed completely.

Having Eyes but Failing to See

Japanese Zen Master Gasan was to cross a river on his way to Daitoku Temple in Kyōto. While he was crossing the river in a ferry, he saw an elderly monk in a straw hat dressed in simple clothing, burying his head in a book reciting *sutras*.

Zen Master Gasan looked at the old monk carefully. He thought to himself, "This monk is old, but he is only on the level of reciting *sutras*. He is probably only a student monk that renounced not long ago."

Zen Master Gasan approached the old monk and said, "Are you taking this ferry to Daitoku Temple?" The old monk lifted his head and replied, "Yes!"

Adopting the attitude of a senior addressing a junior, Zen Master Gasan said, "I think you should go meet Zen Master Kasan. Zen Master Kasan's Zen methods are difficult to learn! Old monk, you are quite old. You should study and cultivate harder, then over time there will be good results."

The old monk listened to Zen Master Gasan's "instructions" quietly with a faint smile on his face.

After the ferry docked, Zen Master Gasan and the old monk traveled together to Daitoku Temple. As they walked, Zen Master Gasan lectured the old monk on the essentials of Zen practice. The old monk listened humbly and politely, attentively taking in all the teachings.

When they arrived at the gates of Daitoku Temple, they saw that the entire monastic community led by the temple's superintendent had come to welcome the old monk, who was the abbot of Daitoku Temple, Zen Master Kasan.

Zen Master Gasan was stunned by the spectacle in front of his eyes. He immediately repented to Zen Master Kasan for his failure to see. Deeply impressed by Zen Master Kasan's magnanimity and broad-mindedness, he decided to become Zen Master Kasan's disciple to study Zen.

There is an idiom: "a full bottle does not move but a half-filled bottle wobbles." Zen Master Gasan had eyes, but failed to see the truth. Zen Master Kasan was an extraordinary individual who was humble and did not show off. Having realized the Way, Zen Master Kasan did not mind that the young man before him failed to see the truth, who was self-righteous, bossy, and ignorant of humility. It was quite fortunate for Zen Master Gasan that he had come upon Zen Master Kasan who was magnanimous and humble! Otherwise he would have been humiliated.

How Can One See the Way?

Chan Master Mǎzǔ Dàoyī's first visit to Chan Master Nányuè Huáiràng occurred during his youth. He asked Chan Master Huáiràng for guidance: "How should I apply my mind in order to attain accord with formless meditative concentration?"

Chan Master Huáiràng told him, "If you want to learn the Dharma method of the mind's field; if you wish to experience or realize the formless *samadhi*, then it's like sowing seeds. It is just like planting seeds; the Dharma is like the rain falling down. Since having planted seeds and rain has also fallen; after some causes and conditions then one day you will certainly see the Way!"

As soon as Chan Master Mǎzǔ Dàoyī heard it described in that way, he continued asking, "Chan Master, you mentioned seeing the Way. What way is there to be seen? The Way is without shape or image. How can we see the Way if it is formless?"

Chan Master Huáiràng replied, "One can see the Way by using the Dharma eye of the mind field. The Way is originally formless meditative concentration. Formless meditative concentration from the mind field allows us to automatically see this Way."

Chan Master Huáiràng was concerned that Chan Master Mǎzǔ would still not understand his question, so he added, "If one attains accord with the Way which has neither beginning nor end, neither arises nor decays, neither gathers nor disperses, neither lengthens nor shortens, neither settled nor chaotic, neither hurried nor delayed, then one can experience the Way."

What is the Way? The Way is not engendered by time. It is without beginning and end. The Way is not engendered by space. It is limitlessly expansive. What is taken as ultimate truth should "transcend qualities of vertical or horizontal orientation throughout the ten directions. As well as transcend delineations of finite and infinite throughout past, present, and future." The Way is everywhere and ubiquitous. How can the Way be understood by us? How can we see the Way? Seeing the Way is understanding one's own ever-abiding true mind. The unchanging true great Way is precisely our own ever-abiding true mind.

Having a mind of compassion is the Way. Having the prajna-wisdom of Chan is the Way. Having a mind set upon the great vow of "I will not seek ease and peace for myself until all beings are able to attain liberation from suffering" is the Way. The Way reaches all places and is everywhere, beyond space and time. It is up to us to figure out how experience it with our Chan minds.

What Auspicious Sign will there be?

During the Northern Song dynasty, Chan Master Chùhuī of Pǔzhào Temple in Sìzhōu became a monk under Chan Master Bǎoníngyǒng in Nánjīng, Jiāngsū. He was the Dharma heir to Chan Master Huìlín Zōngběn, and later in life was appointed to serve as the abbot of Pǔzhào Temple.

When Chan Master Pǔzhào Chùhuī was installed as the new abbot, large assemblies of monks gathered. Many came to attend the ceremony and pay their respects. An endless flow of visitors were coming and going in and around the temple.

That day, Chan Master Pǔzhào Chùhuī went to the main shrine to speak the Dharma. One student monk put forth a question: "Venerable head monk, I heard that time when the Buddha taught the *Lotus Sūtra* the Many Treasure Buddha Stupa sprang up from the earth, which was incomparably auspicious. Great monk, today you are installed as the new abbot and speak the Dharma. Are there any auspicious signs?"

Chan Master Pǔzhào Chùhuī heard this and faintly smiled, "White clouds drift across the sky while flowers on earth sway in the wind. Tell me, are these not auspicious signs?"

The student monk replied, "Those are natural phenomena; they would have nothing to do with your installation today!"

Chan Master Pǔzhào Chùhuī answered, "You are talking and I am listening. Is that not adequately auspicious?"

When he heard this, the student monk felt ashamed and had some realizations.

Auspicious signs are extraordinary occurrences or supernatural manifestations. In truth, isn't the universe full of such events? With a sip of tea, thirst is quenched. With a bowl of rice, hunger is satisfied. Is that not extraordinary? Swimmers can float on water, and climbers can reach tall peaks. Is that not amazing?

Within the Dharma, there are no fantastical events, only one's ordinary mind. Winter, spring, summer, and fall; birth, old age, sickness, and death... all of these are ordinary, worldly phenomena. Since the student monk was unable to accept these unique occurrences in nature, Chan Master Pǔzhào Chùhuī explained to him, "You are talking and I am listening. Is that not auspicious?" Simple as this may seem, this is the wonder of the Dharma!

Where is the Mountain and River?

During the Ming dynasty, Chan Master Zhànrán Yuánchéng of the Cáodòng School received ordination from Chan Master Yúnqī Zhūhóng. He had resided in many temples, such as Yuánchéng Wànshòu Temple, Jiāxìng Dongta Temple, Yúnmén Xiǎnshèng Temple, Nánjīng Yánshòu Temple, and Shàoxīng Huáyán Temple.

One day, a group of lay Buddhists, including Lǚ Jùwú and Zhū Jiāolú came to visit the Chan Master. They gathered in the guest hall to discuss Buddhist *sutras* and one of the lay Buddhists asked, "In Buddhism, it is believed that all phenomena in the world such as mountains, rivers, and the earth itself all originate due to deluded thought. Is that correct?"

Chan Master Zhànrán Yuánchéng answered, "It is indeed so."

The layperson asked, "Given that deluded thoughts can produce all myriad phenomena in the world, could a monk such as yourself think a bar of gold into existence?"

Chan Master Zhànrán Yuánchéng replied, "Okay, I'm done thinking."

The layperson continued, "Venerable monk, since you're done, could you please take it out and show it to us?"

Chan Master Zhànrán Yuánchéng asked the layperson in return, "Have you ever had the experience while in quietude, images of the pavilions, terraces, people, and roads in Hángzhōu come up in your mind?"

The layperson responded, "Yes!"

The Chan Master continued, "As you think of it, do you see the various pavilions and people on the streets in Hángzhōu as clearly as though they are right before your eyes?"

The layperson answered, "Of course!"

Chan Master Zhànrán Yuánchéng abruptly stuck his hands out in front of the layman and remarked, "If so, why don't you take those things out and show them to this monk?"

On hearing this, the layperson's eyes got big and stammered, "What... you've said may be true, but thinking is just thinking, having me pull objects out of them would be completely impossible!"

Chan Master Zhànrán Yuánchéng laughed as he concluded, "Given that you can't take them out to show us, how is it that you ask me to show you a gold bar?"

Within the Dharma, there are principles and phenomena. Our mind may contain the entire trichiliocosm (universe) or the whole world may be included in our mind. In the Dharma it is expressed, "One contains many, and many is but one" or "the Three Realms are within the mind and all myriad phenomena is within the consciousness." This is the "principle," but principles cannot represent "phenomena." Phenomenal forms are unique in their formation; principles and phenomena should not be confused for one another.

In Confucianism, there is a saying, "Look but don't see, listen but don't hear." Even if one looks or listens, if one does not employ proper attention and focus, then what can one accomplish? If we used wisdom, compassion, and resolve to construct a building, then would not such a building be imbued with our wisdom and resolve? If we used these qualities to produce new kinds of computers, cars, and other things throughout the world, then would it not be the case that our mental formations and consciousness be infused worldwide?

That is why we say that the mind is able to penetrate space and time, containing within it all variety of phenomena.

What a Good Sangha Hall

One day, Chan Master Huánglóng Huìnán took his disciple Chan Master Lóngqìng Qìngxián to tour the newly constructed sangha hall. After the inspection, Chan Master Huìnán praised the site, "What a good sangha hall!"

Chan Master Qìngxián heard this, and repeated his words in agreement, "What a good sangha hall!"

Chan Master Huìnán looked at Chan Master Qìngxián and asked, "Well, tell me: what exactly is good about the sangha hall?"

Chan Master Qìngxián answered, "Teacher look, every beam and column in this building is perfectly connected, like the unbroken transmission of the Dharma, a flame passing from lamp to lamp."

Chan Master Huìnán shook his head and countered, "Wrong. That is not why this is a good sangha hall."

Chan Master Qìngxián asked with curiosity, "Well then, Master, what do you think is good?"

Chan Master Huìnán pointed to a column and explained, "Look here: this column is round whereas that column is flat. What is the meaning?"

Chan Master Qìngxián replied, "Whether a column is round, square or flat, they are all similar to human life. Their differing causes and conditions bring different results. This is a profound matter. Only you would be able to explain it, Master."

As they talked, they came outside the hall. Chan Master Huìnán suddenly stopped walking and asked Chan Master Qìngxián, "In the future, after you attain enlightenment, how will you guide sentient beings?"

Chan Master Qìngxián replied seriously, "I will be just as the columns are. When met with squareness, I will be square. When met with roundness, I will be round. Depending on the capacity of the individual, I will teach the Dharma accordingly."

Chan Master Huánglóng Huìnán nodded in approval and praised Chan Master Qìngxián, "Very good! You are already able to flexibly apply the essence of the Dharma."

Once a monastery is constructed, its form is set, but seeing this is just the surface. Where then lay the function? Chan Master Huánglóng Huìnán asked the student monk why there were both round and flat columns. He meant to indicate the columns not only conveyed the Dharma, but also accommodated individuals of differing capacities. The student monk finally understood what his master was saying. The Buddha Hall was not meant to merely enshrine iconography, and the monastery was not meant to merely house monastics. Their main function was to propagate the Dharma and benefit beings. It acts like a waystation, providing food and water for weary travelers. It is a place of recuperation for all sentient beings. That is the function of a sangha hall.

Quiet Sitting for Just a Moment

There was once a monk who sat in meditation upon a bridge when he heard two ghosts talking.

Ghost A remarked to ghost B, "Let me tell you some good news I have: tomorrow someone will come and replace me as a ghost here."

Ghost B responded, "That's great. What does your replacement look like?"

Ghost A answered, "He is just some guy who wears an iron hat."

The monk heard this and decided he would wait for this person to arrive.

Later on, a man wearing an iron wok on his head came jogging under the bridge in the rain. Just as he was preparing to wash his feet in the river, the monk rushed over to tell him what he had overheard. The monk's intervention prevented an accident from occurring and saved the man's life.

Ghost A saw how the monk had ruined something good for him and grew angry. He wanted to harm the monk. The monk immediately sat down in meditation, focused his mind, and entered into meditative concentration.

The two ghosts searched all around but were unable to find the monk. They cried out, "That's strange! Where did he go? Why is there suddenly a jeweled pagoda here?"

After some time had passed, the monk thought to himself, "I bet the ghosts have left by now." He exited meditative concentration, and immediately heard the ghosts called out, "Oh! So he is here!"

Again, the monk hurriedly focused his mind and entered into meditative concentration.

The ghost remarked, "How is it that there is a jeweled pagoda here again? And where did that monk go?"

In this manner, the monk entered and exited meditative concentration three times and achieved a profound enlightenment.

Due to the ghosts' threats and menacing, the monk had accomplished his practice of the Way and became known as Chan Master Guǐ Bī (Harassed by Ghosts).

Virtuous ancients said, "If someone practices sitting quietly for just a moment, the merit gained is superior to that of offering seven-jeweled pagodas as numerous as the grains of sand in the Ganges. Jeweled pagodas will ultimately be reduced to dust, but a quiet thought can lead to enlightenment." So no matter how much merit is garnered through tangible accomplishments, it pales in comparison to the merit gained through a brief moment of quiet meditation, temporarily extinguishing all thoughts of greed, anger, and ignorance in the mind. Even if innumerable jeweled pagodas as many as there are grains of sand in the Ganges River, it would still not equal the merit gained from a single thought of a calm mind engaged in cultivation.

Human existence within the hustle-bustle of this world involves constant work, causing fatigue to mind and spirit. There is tremendous value in finding time each day to sit quietly for chaotic emotions to subside and one's spirit to attain serenity and purity.

Do not Follow the Ancient Path

Chan Master Shimgwan from Korea had talent in scriptural teachings and literary studies. In his youth, he decided to commit himself to studying the *sutras* under Chinese Chan Master Dàjué and to become a follower of Fó Guāng order.

When Chan practitioner Shimgwan first traveled to Mount Báită to pay his respects to Chan Master Dàjué who took one look at him and immediately asked, "Where are you from?"

Chan practitioner Shimgwan respectfully answered, "This student before you has come from the ancient path."

As soon as he heard this, Chan Master Dàjué inquired, "Well, did you see any ancients on your way?"

Chan practitioner Shimgwan replied honestly: "No, I didn't see any ancients."

Chan Master Dàjué asked further, "Since you did not see any ancients, then why are you following their path?"

Chan practitioner Shimgwan found himself unable to understand what Chan Master Dàjué meant; so he just asked back, "May I please ask: what path should I follow then?"

Chan Master Dàjué answered, "You should follow your own path."

After hearing that, Chan practitioner Shimgwan experienced an awakening in his mind, and continued by asking Chan Master Dàjué. "What is one's own path?"

Chan Master Dàjué answered, "The living path of the current times."

This phrase struck Chan practitioner Shimgwan's ears and woke him like a splash of cold water. He immediately joined his palms in respect and bowed before Chan Master Dàjué. From that point on he studied contentedly under Chan Master Dàjué. He spread the Dharma, benefited beings, and received the essential Dharma teachings from him.

The ancient path is the tradition. If a Chan practitioner always hides within tradition, he will have no means to distinguish himself or come into his own. As a Chan practitioner he should walk his own path within his current times. What Chan Master Dàjué was alluding to was the Humanistic Buddhism of our times.

If one only practices sitting meditation and contemplation within meditation halls, but fails to shoulder the responsibility of helping the multitude of sentient beings before their eyes, then can they truly be considered Chan practitioners? If they do not attempt to free others from suffering and hardships and do not stop to consider the needs of others within contemporary society, can they truly be counted among Chan practitioners?

Do Not Take Another as Your Master

Prior to achieving enlightenment, Chan Master Niútóu Făróng practiced on Mount Niútóu in Jiāngsū Province. He would often reside in deep states of meditative concentration. Because he was so focused in his practice, he often ignored the human affairs that occurred around him. When people passed by him, he never paid any attention to them, so much so that people began calling him, "Lănróng (Lazy-róng)" instead of "Făróng."

One day, the Fourth Patriarch, Chan Master Dàoxìn, was passing through Mount Niútóu. He saw that Chan Master Niútóu Făróng was diligent in his practice of meditative concentration so he advised him, "Meditative concentration and enlightenment are not directly related to one another. Entering into this state of stale quiescence will not enable you to connect with the nature of emptiness. You should know that whether it's walking, standing, sitting, lying down, raising your eyebrow, or even within a glance, these are all the magnificent truth of wisdom. These are all the marvelous functions by all buddhas!" Chan Master Niútóu Făróng heard these words and was suddenly enlightened.

A student monk took this encounter between Niútóu Făróng and the Fourth Patriarch Chan Master Dàoxìn to ask Chan Master Tóuzi Dàtóng of Shūzhōu, "Before Master Niútóu Făróng met the Fourth Patriarch Chan Master Dàoxìn, what state had he reached?"

Chan Master Tóuzi Dàtóng replied, "Taking a person as his master."

The student monk asked further, "After the meeting, what was his state?"

Chan Master Tóuzi Dàtóng smiled faintly and then answered, "After they met, he never took a person as his master."

Chan is not in sitting nor meditative concentration. Chan is the use of one's Chan mind in daily life. It is not focusing solely on meditative concentration, and definitely not ignoring everything. Prior to his awakening, Chan Master Niútóu Fǎróng over-committed himself to meditative concentration. It appeared as though his cultivation was accomplished, but in truth, it had plateaued at a state of worldly concentration. After Chan Master Niútóu Fǎróng achieved awakening, he understood that everyone has Buddha Nature. Sentient beings and buddha are non-dual and equal. So when he spread the teachings to liberate the masses, he would not consider himself the teacher. Because sentient beings are only deluded on a thought; they are unable to self-realize and they need benevolent Dharma friends to guide them. In reality, every person has the potential to self-teach and self-realize!

Where is the Head Monk?

Chan Master Huángbò Xīyùn called upon one of his disciples, Chan Master Línjì Yìxuán, to deliver a letter to a fellow Dharma contemporary, Chan Master Wéishān Língyòu. Chan Master Wéishān Língyòu instructed one of his own disciples, Chan Master Yǎngshān Huìjì, to go receive the letter.

Chan Master Yǎngshān later on asked Venerable Línjì, "Given that this letter was written by Chan Master Huángbò, might I please ask you, Head Monk Línjì: where is that letter now?"

Venerable Línjì heard this question and quickly replied, "Didn't I already give the letter to you?" The two of them both engaged in Chan debate and when they finished conversing, they both went to see Chan Master Wéishān Língyòu.

Chan Master Wéishān asked Venerable Línjì, "Exactly how many disciples does Chan Master Huángbò have?"

Venerable Línjì answered, "Seven hundred."

"Out of that group, who among them could assume the role of head monk?"

Venerable Línjì stated, "Just now I asked Dharma brother Yǎngshān to give you a letter."

Only then did Chan Master Yǎngshān pick up the letter. He then remarked, "The letter is here, but where is the head monk?"

At this, Venerable Línjì asked back to Chan Master Wéishān, "May I please ask: how many monastics are here?"

Chan Master Wéishān Língyòu answered, "We have one thousand five hundred monastics here."

Venerable Línjì quipped, "Wow! That really is a lot of people!"

Chan Master Wéishān replied, "Well, your teacher Huángbò also has many disciples."

"Since you have so many people. Could you perhaps return a head monk to us?" Venerable Línjì asked.

Chan Master Wéishān did not respond, and ordered Venerable Yǎngshān to accompany Venerable Línjì back to his temple.

As they walked, Venerable Yǎngshān said to Venerable Línjì, "You should go to the north. You might be able to find a head monk there."

"Could that sort of thing happen?" Venerable Línjì asked skeptically.

Venerable Yǎngshān immediately answered, "You should go anyways! Head monks can recognize other head monks, but non-head monks will not be able to tell. However, I fear a so-called head monk may have a head but lack a tail, be with a beginning but without an end."

Later on, Chan Master Línjì would travel to Zhènzhōu, where he met Chan Master Pǔhuà. When Chan Master Línjì decided to build a monastery, he invited Chan Master Pǔhuà to assist him by assuming the role of head monk. However, just as Venerable Línjì's teachings were flourishing, Chan Master Pǔ Huà died as a result of various causes and conditions.

Chan masters are enlightened to human affairs; they do not take refuting others as their main endeavor. Instead they are deeply concerned for others, and they emphasize receiving students with a heart of compassion. This way of teaching is very subtle and it is up to the student to appreciate the meanings.

Just False, Just True

Chan Master Cáoshān Běnjì of the Tang dynasty was born in Quánzhōu, Fújiàn, and his secular family name was Huáng. He studied the classical teachings of Confucius and Mencius in his youth. At age nineteen, he became a monk under Monk Yuanxiu in Cuìshí Monastery at Mount Língshí, Fúzhōu and became fully ordained at age twenty-five. Around 860 CE, the winds of Chan were flourishing. Chan Master Cáoshān Běnjì came to Pǔlì Temple in Yífēng county, Jiāngxī to pay respects to Chan Master Dòngshān Liángjià. The two forged a deep relationship from their verbal exchanges.

After receiving the Dharma, Běnjì went to bid Dòngshān farewell. While traveling, he arrived in Cáoxī in Guǎngdōng where he paid homage to the pagoda of the Sixth Patriarch Venerable Master Huìnéng. He then returned to Jíshuǐ county in Fúzhōu, Jiāngxī province where he expounded the Dharma. He changed his name to "Cáoshān" to express his sentiment for Cáoxī, many students came to learn from him. Afterwards, the Chan schools of Dòngshān and Cáoshān both flourished and their adherents grew with each passing day, and the Cáodòng School was established. *The Recorded Sayings of Chan Master Cáoshān Běnjì* and commentaries written on *The Poetry of Hán Shānzi* were among the works from this school.

One day, a student monk asked Chan Master Cáoshān Běnjì, "Eyebrows and eyes both grow on the face. Do they know each other?"

Chan Master Cáoshān Běnjì answered, "No, they don't!"

The young monk followed up with, "But they are so close to each other. How could they not know one another?"

Chan Master Cáoshān Běnjì replied, "People may face one another, but minds are separated by thousands of miles."

Not understanding, the monk again asked, "Then how do people come to know each other?"

Chan Master Cáoshān Běnjì shook his head saying, "Eyebrows protect the eyes and eyes show the function of the eyebrows. Because there's one, there's the other; just true, just false... isn't that knowing one another?"

Once the student monk heard this, he experienced an awakening.

Although the eyes are separated, they can see the same view. The nostrils can exhale together, and the ears function the same. The eyebrows may be mistaken as useless, but in fact, they protect the eyes. The eyes merit great importance; the wisdom eyes and Dharma eyes allow people to differentiate between various matters. From their differences, all phenomena return to oneness. They help the true mind in achieving liberation!

Attached to Neither Buddha Nor Māra

Chan Master Xiàng Mózàng's secular family name was Wáng, a native of Héběi, and he became a monk at the age of seven. He was tonsured by Chan Master Míng Zàn of Guăngfú Monastery, a prominent monk during the Tang dynasty. Due to his frequent efforts to eliminate misfortune and superstitions in his village, people honored him with the moniker, "The *Māra*-subduing Chan Master (Chan Master Xiàng Mó)."

During the Northern Song dynasty, the Northern School of Chan Buddhism became prevalent. Chan Master Xiàng Mó decided to go pay his respects to the great masters of the Northern School. One day, Chan Master Xiàng Mó paid a visit to the renowned Chan Master Yùquán Shénxiù.

Chan Master Yùquán Shénxiù asked, "Your name means 'conqueror of *Māra*,' but I have no mountain demons or forest goblins here. Since there are no *māras* to conquer here, could it be that you have come as a *māra*?"

Chan Master Xiàng Mó spoke with great certainty, "If there are buddhas, then there are *māras*. I am a *māra* too!"

Chan Master Yùquán Shénxiù noted that what he said was remarkable and went a step further by asking him, "If you are a *māra*, then you must be a *māra* of an extraordinary state."

Unflinching, Chan Master Xiàng Mó replied, "Even if we were talking about buddhas rather than *māras*, their self-nature would likewise be empty. What state could manifest?"

Upon hearing this, Chan Master Yùquán Shénxiù realized that Chan Master Xiàng Mó was a Dharma vessel. He made a prediction: "Your Dharmic conditions lay in the region of Shǎohào an area around Mount Tài. In the future, you will deliver countless sentient beings there."

Chan Master Xiàng Mó later moved to the Eastern Summit of Mount Tài to spread the Dharma. In merely a few short years, an endless stream of student monks would come to him to inquire about the Way.

This world is one of halves: half daytime, half nighttime; half wholesome people, half wicked people; half buddhas, half māras. Buddhas and māras occur within a thought. An enlightened thought is a buddha, and a deluded thought is a māra. A pure thought unswayed by mundane states is a buddha state.

However, Chan Master Zhàozhōu Cóngshěn once remarked, "Do not seek to remain forever in buddha state, but also pass through non-buddha states quickly." Even if one encounters a buddha state, one should still avoid giving rise to thoughts of attachment and craving. There is a saying, "If māras come, behead them. If buddhas come, behead them." If the mind has no attainment for buddhas or māras, then one will naturally be liberated with no obstacles.

Not Wanting One's Inheritance

One day, Chan Master Bǎizhàng Huáihǎi was expounding the Dharma to his disciples and concluded by mentioning: "The Dharma is not some trifling matter. This old monk once went to Chan Master Mǎzǔ Dàoyī for instruction. He shouted at me so loudly that I was struck blind and deaf for three days and three nights."

Chan Master Huángbò Xīyùn heard this and stuck out his tongue in response. Chan Master Bǎizhàng caught sight of this and remarked, "Perhaps you do not wish to inherit the Dharma of Patriarch Mǎzǔ Dàoyī's Chan teachings?"

Chan Master Huángbò replied, "No, it's not that. After hearing your words tonight, I was able to see the Patriarch's great facility and great functionality, however, it is fortunate that I did not have the opportunity to meet him. It is best that we don't meet."

Chan Master Bǎizhàng looked at him and asked, "Why don't you want to meet him? You're his Dharma-heir. In the future you will inherit the Dharma of his Chan teachings."

Chan Master Huángbò replied, "I don't want to inherit them."

Chan Master Bǎizhàng asked, "Why not?"

Chan Master Huángbò responded, "Whether or not I am able to inherit the Dharma of the Patriarch is not up to me to decide."

Chan Master Bǎizhàng nodded his head and cracked a faint smile upon hearing this. He commented, "But it is also not up to you to refuse."

Chan Master Huángbò then placed his palms together and bowed in reverence.

Chan Master Bǎizhàng soon after remarked, "Great facility and great functionality."

Chan Master Huángbò also replied with: "Great facility and great functionality."

Among the Chan gōng'àns, the case of "One shout from Mǎzǔ deafened Bǎizhàng for three days" is well-known. From this anecdote, we can see Mǎzǔ Dàoyī's brash Sichuanese behavior. In Chan Master Bǎizhàng we see the cautiousness of the Fujianese. That is why there is the saying that "Mǎzǔ founded forest monasteries; Bǎizhàng established pure rules."

Chan Master Huángbò Xīyùn inherited the Chan methods of Chan Master Mǎzǔ Dàoyī. Most consider him as having surpassed Chan Master Bǎizhàng in this regard. Later on, he and Chan Master Línjì Yìxuán became two of the foundational masters who pioneered the skillful usage of discipline rods and awakening shouts. This is just like the "great facility and great functionality" that Chan Master Bǎizhàng spoke of. Chan Master Huángbò too did not hesitate to assume responsibilities and sustain "great facility and great functionality" in teaching.

Having No Interest in Possessing

Chan Master Yǒudào practiced a unique style of Chan. He did not accept disciples and avoided audiences. He was only attended by a monk who had followed him since the age of fifteen. They lived together leisurely for over twenty years, spending a simple life together. The old master did not lecture his attendant on *sutras* nor deliver formal lessons. His attendant just brought him food to eat and tea to drink, spending their days together in this ordinary way.

One cold winter, the old master felt that his time was coming. He summoned his only attendant and asked him, "How many years have you been serving this old monk?"

His attendant respectfully answered, "I do not remember how many years it's been."

Chan Master Yǒudào remarked, "Indeed, in the mountains one knows not the passage of time. Excellent, excellent!"

As he spoke, Chan Master Yǒudào carefully placed a Dharma scroll upon the table. He continued, "All the years we've spent together, I have given you nothing. This book was handed to me by my own master. I am the seventh generation to receive it, and now I pass it on to you."

His attendant responded, "Master, keep it for yourself. There's no need to pass it on to me."

Chan Master Yǒudào insisted, "I am old now. It would be a pity if I did not pass this on." As he said this, he handed the book to his attendant, and remarked, "Keep it well, keep it well."

His attendant received the Dharma scroll respectfully with two hands. Abruptly, he deposited the scroll into the stove beside him. In the raging flames, the scroll was quickly reduced to ash and smoke.

Chan Master Yǒudào cried out with eyes wide open, "What are you doing?"

Unperturbed, his attendant answered, "What are you saying?"

The two looked at one another and erupted into laughter.

Chan Master Yǒudào and his attendant had maintained a master-student relationship for many years. Although they exchanged few words, it was clear they spoke the Dharma to each other every day. Without the more than twenty years together, without the incinerating of the Dharma scroll, and without their shared laughter, how could their minds have been in accord? The way of masters and their students in Chan Buddhism is truly marvelous!

What is Most Painful?

One day, Chan Master Dòngshān Liángjià asked a group of student monks, "What do you think is the most painful thing in the world?"

One immediately replied, "Hell is the most painful thing of all!"

Chan Master Dòngshān Liángjià answered, "Not necessarily."

Another monk spoke up, "Being bound by emotions is most painful."

Chan Master Dòngshān Liángjià still answered, "Not necessarily."

Yet another monk said, "Bodily aging and sickness are the most painful."

Chan Master Dòngshān Liángjià shook his head and replied, "The forms of suffering you mentioned have methods to overcome them, so they are not the most painful phenomena in the world."

At that time, a monk cautiously asked, "Master, what do you take to be the most painful thing?"

"To not understand the main concern from underneath these robes. That is the most painful thing." Chan Master Dòngshān Liángjià said with emphatic intention.

"Underneath these robes" refers to Buddhist monks who wear the robes (kāṣāya) in practicing the Way. "To not understand the main concern" means to not understand the main concern of life and death. Chan Master Dòngshān Liángjià clearly taught the Dharma that the issue of birth and death cannot be resolved. "Not understanding this main concern" is the most painful phenomenon in the world.

The Chan School of Buddhism has a saying, "If one does not understand birth and death, one suffers as if they've lost their parents." Chan patriarchs frequently used "the main concern of life and death" to goad practitioners to realize the swiftness of impermanence. It helps prevent their minds from becoming deluded by superficial and unsubstantial external states. They learn to treasure what they have around them, take life seriously in the present moment, and not allow thoughts to wander.

Life and death are the two greatest lessons in life. The proverb "Your own life and death are yours alone to resolve" indicates that no one can face these matters for you. You must face them by yourself. In life, strive to live freely, completely, and meaningfully. At death, have peace of mind, let go, without regret, and go without attachments. In this manner, whether it is life or death, one is able to be free and peaceful.

Go to Hell

For those who wish to study Chan, Chan Buddhism always encourages them to contemplate on critical phrases (*huàtóu*). They are various questions and reflections such as "Who is reciting the Buddha's name?" "What was my original face before my parents gave birth to me?" "What is the intention of the Patriarch Bodhidharma coming from the West?" These questions aim to trigger one's spiritual nature, leading to great awakenings.

One devotee asked Chan Master Zhàozhōu Cóngshěn, "Chan Master, you are a Chan master of great enlightenment, regularly practicing Chan, studying the Way, cultivating wisdom and merit, and have gained perfection of character, where will you be going after you pass away?" The devotee hoped that Chan Master Zhàozhōu Cóngshěn would tell everyone when he was still alive about which Buddha land or heaven he would go to in the future.

It never occurred to him that Master Zhàozhōu would answer by saying, "I'll go to hell."

The devotee was very shocked and then asked, "Chan Master, given your cultivation and virtuous behavior, how could it be that you would fall into hell after you pass away?"

Chan Master Zhàozhōu answered, "You should know that the negative karma accumulated through acts of killing, stealing, sexual misconduct, false speech; and other such transgressions with your greed, anger, and ignorance will cause you to fall into hell. So if I don't go to hell, then who is going to liberate you? Who's going to save you?"

Chan Master Zhàozhōu wanted to go to hell, his spirit is the same as that of Kṣitigarbha Bodhisattva. Those with negative karma have no choice but to go to hell, but those of deep cultivation and great vows go to hell on the strength of their vows. The hell they go to is the same, but whether it is going there due to their negative karma or on the strength of their vow to liberate sentient beings is not the same. Whether it is Kṣitigarbha Bodhisattva or Chan Master Zhàozhōu Cóngshěn, they both have unlimited compassion, bringing the vastness of their practice and vows to hell to liberate beings from suffering and hardship. This is the meaning of the words, "If I do not enter hell, then who will?"

When it comes to liberating sentient beings, we should not necessarily go to wealthy places, well-populated places, or places where we can easily liberate others. True Chan practitioners on the Way and bodhisattvas in liberating sentient beings all uphold: "the more suffering there is in a place, the more I wish to go. The more hardship there is by conditions, the more I wish to go." It is just like why all bodhisattvas wish to come to the saha world to attain Buddhahood. That is because the saha world is a world of the five defilements. Cultivating the Way from within this world makes realization less difficult. Those who practice Chan and study the Way should follow the words of Venerable Master Cí Háng, "So long as even a single person has yet to be delivered, one should never run away."

Where Can One Safely Abide?

One day, Chan Master Dānxiá Tiānrán went to visit Chan Master Mǎzǔ Dàoyī. On the way there, he came across a gray bearded older man and a young boy.

Chan Master Dānxiá noticed that there was something transcendent about the old man. He went before the old man and respectfully asked, "Sir, may I please ask where you live?"

The old man did not immediately reply. Instead he pointed to the sky, then he pointed toward the earth. He then replied "The heavens above and the earth below." Thereby displaying that he considered the whole universe to be his home.

Chan Master Dānxiá asked further, "After the destruction of heaven and earth, where will you live?"

The old man roared loudly, "The blue sky! The blue sky!" This meant that the universe has always been subject to formation, abiding, decaying, and extinction.

The young boy offered a "hmmph" from beside them. It was a gesture associated with revealing one's original nature. The original nature is subject to neither arising nor cessation. Heaven and earth may one day cease to be, but one's original nature does not cease.

Upon hearing this, Chan Master Dānxiá stopped to offer great praise: "Father lions do not sire canine puppies!"

Venerable Master Cí Háng, famed for leaving behind a relic body that did not decay, once said, "One only needs to self-awaken to the tranquility of the mind. Any direction, north, south, east or west is good." Therefore, there is no home to be found on earth or in heaven, but everywhere can serve as home. Worldly people live among sensuality, commercial gain, reputation, wealth, power, and love. All these things change unceasingly. Upon which of those phenomena can we safely abide?

If people resolve to not be led by the five desires and six sense objects to gain the ability to have their minds abide in still serenity and satisfaction, then what more is to be done regarding the collapse of heaven and earth. "Bodhisattvas continuously travel through the emptiness just as the moon drifts through the sky." The moon exists in empty space. It seems there is nothing upon which it can depend and as such is in a state of extreme danger. However, actually it abides safely within this empty space. This is because bodhisattvas always abide within the empty nature of prajñā. They are without hindrance, and that is why a bodhisattva lives in a state of freedom and ease. As long as we have Chan, then life will be in freedom and ease.

The Truly Ill

Zen Master Bankei Eitaku was born in 1622 and passed away in 1693. He was a native of Harima province (present day Hyōgo prefecture), Japan. He practiced Confucianism in his early life, but became a monk at the age of seventeen and he traveled to different places to study Zen. At age twenty-six he attained the essence of Zen Master Bokuō Sogyū's Dharma, inheriting the lineage of the Rinzai School. He established Zen temples and renovated Zen monasteries, accepting over four hundred disciples.

Often, Zen Master Bankei joyfully taught Zen for officials and commoners alike. He emphasized that all people had Zen minds and Buddha nature. He taught that Zen is not just seated meditation, it neither arises nor ceases but exists within our daily lives. It was called "Non-Arising Zen."

During Zen Master Bankei's time as an abbot, he led the assembly in cultivation, and treated all with equality and compassion. Zen Master Bankei gave ten year old novice monks dinner, exempted fifty year old monks from labor, and granted seventy year old monks private rooms. If people fell ill, Zen Master Bankei treated them all equally and cared for them in the recovery hall, regardless of whether they were his personal disciples or traveling students.

He appointed his disciple Settei as the caregiver of that hall. Since the temple was crowded and busy, some people felt overwhelmed by the labor and activities, and they made excuses to rest in the recovery hall.

One monk complained about this to Settei, "Some of these people are just slackers who are pretending to be sick to get out of working."

Another monk said, "These sorts of people are a blight on the temple. They must be driven out of here."

Yet another monk chimed in, "Slackers are the truly ill here!"

Rumors began to spread. One after another, people came to complain to Zen Master Settei.

Zen Master Settei replied, "I am following the Master's orders, I cannot evict them without good reason."

Still another monk said, "Are you following his orders when you care for those 'patients' who resent practice?"

Zen Master Settei did not know how to reply and went to the abbot Zen Master Bankei, for help.

Hearing what had happened, Zen Master Bankei replied lightly, "Any problems with the body are an illness. Laziness is an illness, resenting practice is an illness, and looking down upon others is an illness. No matter the case, how not to be ill is of utmost importance."

The assembly heard these words and each reflected with shame. Since then, they practiced diligently, and their cultivation of the Way was revitalized.

In Christianity's "New Testament," there is an anecdote wherein a women commits adultery. By law, she was to be stoned to death. Jesus said to the onlookers, "Let he who is without sin cast the first stone." Ashamed, on hearing this the crowd dispersed quietly.

Here we see Zen Master Bankei question his noisy followers: Who among you is not ill? If everyone were sound of body and mind, then naturally they will be well with no need for medicine.

Where is My Ailment?

During the Southern Song dynasty, Chan Master Huì'ān Míguāng was a Dharma heir of Chan Master Dàhuì Zōnggǎo from the Línjì School of Chan. For a time, Chan Master Huì'ān Míguāng served at Yunmen Monastery as Chan Master Dàhuì Zōnggǎo's attendant, taking care of the Chan Master.

One day, Huì'ān Míguāng asked the old master, "Chan Master, I have stayed here for some time now, but I remain unable to understand my own Chan mind. Where is my ailment?"

Chan Master Dàhuì Zōnggǎo spent much of his time together with Huì'ān Míguāng, he could see what was wrong with him in a glance. With a face of mild frustration he explained, "Your ailment has long infected deep into you, no doctors in the world can help you. This so-called ailment is ignorance and delusion, a form of darkness; how could they connect with the brightness of the Dharma?"

Confused, Huì'ān Míguāng asked, "How is that so? How does one rid oneself of ignorance and delusion to come to know one's Chan mind?"

"Others have died and cannot come back alive. You are alive and have yet to die." Chan Master Dàhuì Zōnggǎo continued with serious composure, "You must experience great death; only then will you attain great ease."

Huì'ān Míguāng still did not understand and his confusion became even greater.

After a few days, Chan Master Dàhuì Zōnggǎo suddenly asked him, "Have you eaten your porridge yet?

Have you gone to wash your alms bowl? Say something for me."

After a few days of contemplation, Huì'ān Míguāng said the word, "Broken."

"Ah!" Chan Master Dàhuì Zōnggǎo suddenly cried out loud, "Why are you speaking of Chan again?"

With this shout, Huì'ān Míguāng attained the clarity of sudden awakening.

There is a saying, "Dispel the clouds to see the sun." Only after Chan Master Huì'ān Míguāng found a method to rid himself of ignorance and worries was he able to utter the word, "broken." Nevertheless, Chan Master Dàhuì Zōnggǎo shouted, "How come you're talking about Chan again?" He feared that Huì'ān Míguāng had not truly made the effort, and was simply reciting words he'd heard. Chan Master Dàhuì reprimanded him, "You're still talking about Chan?" This enabled Chan Master Huì'ān Míguāng to achieve sudden awakening and finally became enlightened.

"Awakening" does not occur through written words, speech, or thought. Awakening points directly to one's original mind; seeing one's nature and thereby awakened. Awakening is not intellectual knowledge; it is not reasoned out through discrimination of thoughts, nor is it a trick of smoke and mirrors. Awakening is opening the gate of one's mind and seeing one's self directly. The word Chan Master Huì'ān Míguāng used, "broken," was an expression of his practice. Chan Master Dàhuì Zōnggǎo's shout furthered the extent of his awakening. It was through this exchange that Chan Master Huì'ān Míguāng finally saw his nature and awakened to the Way.

Not One's Own Treasure

Chan Master Cáoshān Guānghuì (also known as Chan Master Héyù Guānghuì), was a Buddhist monk during the Tang dynasty. He was a Dharma heir of Chan Master Cáoshān Běnjì. Chan Master Cáoshān Guānghuì served at Lóngquán, but later came to spread the Dharma at Mount Héyù (Cáoshān) in Fǔzhōu.

One day, a student monk came to study at Chan Master Cáoshān Guānghuì's temple. Upon seeing Chan Master Cáoshān Guānghuì, the student monk remarked, "I have brought my own treasure, a precious piece of un-carved jade, to learn from you."

Hearing his words, Chan Master Cáoshān Guānghuì looked him over carefully, unimpressed, sighed and said, "If it is something you were allowed to carry around wherever you go, then it is not really your treasure. How can you call such a thing precious?"

The student monk heard this and felt quite ashamed. He bowed respectfully and said, "In that case, Master, please compassionately teach me what counts as my own treasure."

Chan Master Cáoshān Guānghuì spoke weightily: "Without carving, jade cannot become a useful vessel."

Here, "uncarved jade" is a metaphor for the Buddha Nature inherent in all people. For our Buddha Nature to be revealed requires a process which can be likened to carving. The jade's rough edges must be smoothed out and its impurities be removed for it to become a truly beautiful gem. We must also go through the process of cultivation to remove our worries and attachments in order to reveal our pure, original self-nature.

The student monk believed that by bringing his own treasure, his intrinsic Buddha Nature (uncarved jade) was sufficient for training and studying. However, without going through study, cultivation, and contemplation, how could his Buddha Nature possibly be revealed? Consequently, Chan Master Cáoshān Guānghuì reprimanded the student monk with "Not your own treasure."

In the resolve for studying the Way, do not look for an effortless practice without obstructions. Without obstruction or trials and tribulations, one is like jade yet to be carved. Only by going through life's tests, difficulties, and cultivating the field of the mind before our true mind and original nature shine forth brightly.

You Do Not Have the Wisdom Eye

Chan Master Dàzhū Huìhǎi whose secular family name was Zhū, was a native of Jiànzhōu (present day Fújiàn) during the Tang dynasty. He took refuge, became a monk, and studied *sutras* and teachings under Chan Master Dào Zhì at Dàyún Temple in Yuèzhōu (Shàoxīng, Zhèjiāng). Later in life, he traveled extensively and went to Jiāngxī to pay respects to Chan Master Mǎzǔ Dàoyī. Upon first seeing him, Chan Master Mǎzǔ Dàoyī asked him, "You do not look after your own family's treasure. What do you hope to do by fleeing your home to wander aimlessly?" On hearing this, Huìhǎi attained great realizations and followed Chan Master Mǎzǔ Dàoyī for six years before returning to Yuèzhōu to widely spread Chan teachings.

One day, a practitioner asked Chan Master Dàzhū Huìhǎi, "Chan Master Mǎzǔ Dàoyī often used the phrase 'the mind is the Buddha' to guide his students. Looking upon all phenomena, I'm not sure which among them can be taken as a buddha."

Upon hearing this, Chan Master Dàzhū Huìhǎi yelled, "You suspect that one of them is not a buddha? Then bring that one forth for us to see!"

Unwilling to appear weak, the practitioner continued, "After the appearance of the Tathāgata Śākyamuni, there were one thousand two hundred fifty great arhats, and eminent monks over the generations. May I ask you Chan Master, which among them was the successor of Śākyamuni Buddha? Were they all buddhas?"

Chan Master Dàzhū Huìhǎi replied, "You've committed a grave transgression. Among all the multitudes of sentient beings, can you say that any one of them is not a buddha?"

The practitioner asked back, "Then how should I use the wisdom eye to recognize which are buddhas?"

Chan Master Dàzhū Huìhǎi looked at the practitioner and said, "What a pity! You do not have a wisdom eye and therefore have no means of knowing about the hundreds of thousands of millions of buddhas."

The practitioner heard this and had a sudden insight. He bowed before the Chan Master Dàzhū Huìhǎi and took his leave.

After the Buddha attained enlightenment, his first proclamation was "Upon this great earth, all sentient beings have Buddha Nature." This already indicated all the multitudes of sentient beings were equal. Buddhas are sentient beings who have already attained enlightenment. Sentient beings are buddhas who have not yet achieved enlightenment. The two differ in terms of time, not nature. Chan Master Dàzhū Huìhǎi flipped the question around on this practitioner and asked him, "Which one is not a buddha?" It is the respect that is due to all individuals; it is the affirmation of Buddha Nature. If all the multitudes of sentient beings are Tathāgata buddhas within our eyes, then how would the present moment be anything other than a buddha land?

I am Still on the Path

Tang dynasty Chan Master Hézé Shénhuì was a native of Xiāngyáng in Húběi province. During his youth, he studied thoroughly the Confucian classics. He was naturally gifted, and later in life, he became interested in Buddhism. He became a monk at Guóchāng Temple under the guidance of Chan Master Hàoyuán.

When Chan Master Hézé Shénhuì was fourteen, he heard that the Sixth Patriarch, Chan Master Huìnéng had come to the south to teach Chan Buddhism, so Shénhuì immediately set out to go see him.

Chan Master Huìnéng saw Shénhuì and decided to test him. He asked Shénhuì, "Where are you from?"

Shénhuì answered, "I do not come from anywhere."

Chan Master Huìnéng asked again, "Since you do not come from anywhere, how will you return?"

Shénhuì answered, "There is nowhere for me to return."

Chan Master Huìnéng shook his head and replied, "The kind of answer that you have given is too vague."

Shénhuì did not back down and composedly responded, "That is because I'm still on the path."

Chan Master Huìnéng lightly remarked, "Was it difficult to have come so far?"

Shénhuì smiled faintly, "Seeing the Patriarch, I have already arrived."

Chan Master Huìnéng returned a slight smile and nodded, accepting Shénhuì's answer. After that, Shénhuì stayed to practice and study under his guidance.

Many people use the metaphor of a path to describe life. They call it the "Path of Life." As soon as we are born, we begin walking the path of life. Reaching one's destination is often a metaphor for the end of a life. On this road, we may traverse mountain and rivers, cross obstacles and other impediments. Or we may find the wind at our backs, our travels smooth and successful. Life has many different faces and aspects.

The Sixth Patriarch asked Shénhuì, "Where are you from?" Shénhuì answered, "I do not come from anywhere." This response was well-suited to the Sixth Patriarch's philosophy. His teachings emphasized "emptiness." In his poem on enlightenment, he stated that "Bodhi is originally without a tree and the clear mirror is likewise without a stand."

Next, Chan Master Huìnéng asked Shénhuì, "How will you return?" Shénhuì answered, "There is nowhere for me to return." This was another proper response to "emptiness." Although Shénhuì was young, he showed great potential. Chan Master Huìnéng agreed to let Shénhuì stay by his side. It was this that led to him becoming a Chan Master for the generations.

At that time, Chan Master Huìnéng from the Southern School and Chan Master Shénxiù from the Northern School were opposed to each other. One was situated in remote Lǐngnán in the south. The other was located in the northern capital and had received royal patronage. After spreading the Way and Dharma for many years, Chan Master Shénhuì organized a great debate in Huátái. There, Chan Master Huìnéng was recognized as the true successor of Chan Buddhism. Therefore, we should never underestimate youth, and the affinity between master and student had led to auspicious causes and conditions within Chan Buddhism.

I Also Have a Wife

Chan Master Wǔzǔ-Shān Fǎyǎn was a native of Sichuan during the Northern Song dynasty. After he was fully ordained at age thirty-five, he traveled to Chengdu to study the *Treatises on One Hundred Dharmas* and other teachings of the Mind-Only School. Later, he turned to Chan, studying under Chan masters such as Huìlín Zōngběn and Fúshān Fǎyuǎn. Finally, he became enlightened under Chan Master Báiyún Shǒuduān, of the Yángqí sect, Línjì school and inherited his Dharma teachings.

After receiving the Dharma, Chan Master Wǔzǔ-Shān Fǎyǎn held successive abbotships on Mount Sìmiàn, Mount Báiyún, and Mount Tàipíng. Afterwards, he moved to teach students at Dōngchán Temple on Mount Wǔzǔ in Qízhōu. Because of his residency at Mount Wǔzǔ, he became known as Wǔzǔ Fǎyǎn. He had many Dharma heirs and students, including Fóyǎn Qīngyuǎn, Fójiàn Huìqín, and Fóguǒ Kèqín. These three became known as the "Three buddhas under Fǎyǎn's tutelage."

One day, a lay devotee came to Mount Wǔzǔ to see Chan Master Fǎyǎn. As soon as they met, the devotee prostrated himself and said, "Chan Master, I have cast aside the entanglements of the mundane world. Please, compassionately accept and allow me to become a monk to study under your guidance."

Chan Master Fǎyǎn looked at him carefully before asking, "How did you go about casting aside your worldly entanglements?"

The devotee replied, "I broke ties with my wife. That is how I renounced all my worldly involvements."

Chan Master Fǎyǎn responded, "In the *Vimalakīrti Sūtra* it says, 'bodhisattvas have wisdom as the mother, skillful means the father, and Dharma joy the wife.' You have a wife, but you don't want her. I don't have a wife, but I'm looking for one."

The devotee was shocked by this. He had never imagined that this great monk would utter such words. He was too surprised to reply.

Chan Master Fǎyǎn laughed as he continued, "In the *Vimalakīrti Sūtra* it also says, 'compassion is one's daughters and wholesomeness and sincerity are one's sons.' Now your household is complete. Why reject your family and search for one here? Who could give them to you?"

The householder heard this, but did not quite understand. Consequently, he did not become a monk, but he did resolve to volunteer at the temple and serve the community.

Those living in the secular world should be responsible in their marriages. From ancient times until present, marriage was not considered temporary, but was instead taken as a lifelong commitment. It does not matter whether one is a man or woman, both should know that being a husband or a wife is a responsibility. Having children is likewise a responsibility. Working hard and dedicating oneself in the world is even more of a responsibility. If you give these things up, and wish to go somewhere else to find another loving family, where would you be able to find one?

It is a shame that there are lay practitioners who lack the Dharma and only think of their own liberation. They wish to give up their families to become monastics. How could such thinking lead to the Way? The Vimalakīrti Sūtra *says, "Bodhisattvas have wisdom as the mother, skillful means the father, Dharma joy the wife, compassion is the daughter, and wholesomeness and sincerity are the son." This is the best situation!*

Personal Matters

Chan Master Tiānzhù Chónghuì was a Tang dynasty monk of the Oxhead School of Chan Buddhism. He became the Dharma heir of Chan Master Niútóu (Oxhead) Zhìwēi, the founding patriarch of Mt. Tiānzhù in Shūzhōu.

One day, a student monk came before Chan Master Tiānzhù Chónghuì seeking instruction. He asked, "Before the Patriarch Bodhidharma had come to China, did China have the Dharma or not?"

Chan Master Tiānzhù Chónghuì replied, "Let's hold off on the matter of China before the arrival of Bodhidharma. First tell me of your current matters."

The student monk did not understand. He said to Chan Master Tiānzhù Chónghuì, "I don't follow your meaning. Chan Master, please, kindly teach me again."

Chan Master Tiānzhù Chónghuì responded lightly, "Enduring emptiness of the universe since ancient times, shifting wind and changing moon in one day."

Chan Master Tiānzhù Chónghuì saw that the student still did not understand. He added, "How do your personal matters have anything to do with the arrival of Bodhidharma? Even if he were here, he is no fortune-teller who could divine your future. Whether fortune or disaster awaits you, they are your business, you should shoulder all the responsibilities yourself!"

What are personal matters? For a beginner practicing Chan, how one folds their legs, how one gives rise to right mindfulness, how one seeks oneself, how one settles oneself; these are all personal matters. However, the question put forth by the student monk had nothing to do with learning Chan. That is why Chan Master Tiānzhù Chónghuì replied, "Timeless and endless is space, but the wind and moon occupy the present day," pointing out the importance of practicality in cultivation. There is no Dharma to be found outside of the here and now.

Chan does not distinguish between past, present, and future; nor is it limited by borders and boundaries; nor is there distinction between self and other or right and wrong. Eternity is contained within an instant; within one thought there are three thousand realms. Only by seizing the here and now, contemplating oneself, then one is complete with the Dharma. There is no reason to seek from outside.

A Fundamental Problem

Initially, Japanese Zen Master Shinkan studied the Tendai (Chinese Tiāntái) teachings for six years, and later on he studied Zen for seven years. Afterwards, he set out on a journey to find a teacher in the pursuit to know his mind, see his nature, and discover his original face. He traveled to China, going to renowned monasteries and temples to engage in *huàtóu* contemplation and study meditative concentration. After twelve years, his practice of Chan allowed him to learn a little more about himself. Afterwards, he packed up and returned to Japan to propagate Zen practice in Kyōto and Nara.

Students from across Japan sought to meet him, fighting for the opportunity to hear his answers to difficult questions such as "What is one's original face?" "Why did Bodhidharma come from the West?" "Do dogs really have Buddha Nature?" Despite being bombarded with questions, Zen Master Shinkan closed his eyes and remained silent.

One day, a student monk in his fifties named Michifumi who had been studying Tendai teachings for thirty years came to see Zen Master Shinkan. With great sincerity he said, "Throughout my youth I studied the philosophy of the Tendai School. However, there was always a question that I have been unable to understand."

Zen Master Shinkan replied, "The Tendai School emphasizes broad, profound thinking, seeking to be harmonious and unobstructed. You should have many questions, yet you claim to have only one unanswered. What is this question?"

Venerable Michifumi answered, "In the *Lotus Sūtra* it says, 'Sentient and insentient beings both attain perfect wisdom.' That means that grasses, flowers, and trees are all able to attain Buddhahood. How can plants attain Buddhahood?"

Zen Master Shinkan replied, "If you spent thirty years contemplating whether or not grasses, flowers, and trees could attain Buddhahood, what benefit would there be for you? Shouldn't you be concerning yourself with whether or not *you* can attain Buddhahood."

Venerable Michifumi was surprised by this response. He returned, "I had not thought of it that way before. Tell me then, how can I go about attaining Buddhahood?"

Zen Master Shinkan answered, "You said you only had one question to ask me. This second question you must answer yourself."

The fields, mountains, rivers, flowers, grasses, trees, and all myriad things in the world all originate from our self-nature. When we achieve Buddhahood, so do all these myriad things. How can one enter into the path of Zen if one neglects to investigate the roots of the matter, but instead searches for where its branches reach? Zen requires recognizing one's present self. One should not cling on to other conditions and phenomena.

A No-Edge Sword

One day, a student monk asked Chan Master Cáoshān Běnjì, "Master, may I ask: what is 'a no-edge sword?'"

Chan Master Cáoshān Běnjì answered, "'A no-edge sword' is a sword that does not require a blacksmith to forge it."

The student monk then asked, "How is a no-edge sword special? How does it differ from regular swords?"

Chan Master Cáoshān Běnjì responded, "With just a touch, it can cut through hundreds of thousands of arrowroot vines."

The student monk asked further, "What should one do if he lacks the necessary affinities to come across a no-edge sword?"

Chan Master Cáoshān Běnjì replied with great certainty, "The arrowroot vines of habitual tendencies can be cut down just the same."

Hearing this, the student monk could not help but wonder aloud, "If one possesses a no-edge sword, then one can chop down all deluded thoughts and attachments. However, how does one cut down their habitual tendencies without coming across the sword?"

Chan Master Cáoshān Běnjì gently answered, "Surely you have heard that no-edge swords can reach anywhere and cut through anything?"

The student monk then asked, "After you slice through all delusions, what state has one reached?"

Chan Master Cáoshān Běnjì laughed heartily and answered, "At that time, you will have a greater understanding of what a no-edge sword is!"

"A no-edge sword" is an analogy for the prajñā-wisdom, which cuts through the delusion and ignorance in the minds of the unenlightened. It is able to eliminate our negative karmic conditions and habitual tendencies, allowing us to gain liberation and ease. Cultivation requires supporting causes and conditions of Dharma friends teaching and guiding us. Then, one may be able to free oneself from the quagmire of ignorance since ancient times. Even without the guidance of Dharma friends, when causes and conditions are ripe, knowing one's mind and seeing one's nature will still be possible. Because our prajñā self-nature is intrinsically pure, there will certainly come the day when liberation from worries is achieved.

In Buddhism, it is said that, "When lost, teachers deliver students; when awakened, students deliver themselves." Even if one is fortunate enough to meet an excellent teacher, one still has to rely upon one's own efforts. Even without a good teacher, if one is able to form wholesome connections while planting seeds of merit, one will find themselves on the Buddhist path, delivering oneself and others.

My Vows are Mine Alone

Once a lay Buddhist who had not studied Buddhism for a particularly long time, began reading *An Inspiration to Give Rise to the Bodhi Mind.* He read the verse, "A diamond is not firm; but the power of a vow is the firmest." Since he did not understand the meaning of this verse, the lay Buddhist went to Chan Master Wúxiāng to request instruction.

Chan Master Wúxiāng said to him, "As a student of Buddhism who is on the path to enlightenment, it is difficult to avoid one's own inertia, karmic hindrances, and other such unfortunate negative qualities which serve as obstacles upon the path. These causes and conditions can deplete one's bodhicitta. That is why it is necessary to rely upon the strength of one's vow for support and encouragement. Among the eminent monks of great virtue over the generations who succeeded upon the path; they all attained enlightenment by relying upon vows without digression. Take for example the ten great vows of Samantabhadra Bodhisattva, the twelve great vows of Avalokitêśvara, the forty-eight great vows of Amitābha Buddha, or the compassionate vow of Kṣitigarbha Bodhisattva who pledged, 'I vow to only achieve Buddhahood after all of the hells have been emptied.' Among these great vows which were pledged by numerous buddhas and bodhisattvas, every vow could be a guide to those who study Buddhism."

The lay Buddhist still could not understand this teaching and thereby asked, "Why is it necessary to resolve liberating sentient beings in order to achieve Buddhahood?"

Chan Master Wúxiāng answered, "This is just like a tree and sentient beings are like the roots of that tree. One must care for them because as soon as the roots have been damaged, the tree will wither and rot. How then could the tree ever come to flower or bear fruit?"

The devotee finally understood the strength which comes from vows. He then asked Chan Master Wúxiāng what the Chan Master's own vows were.

Chan Master Wúxiāng replied, "My vows are my own. They are not yours. Why don't you make some vows of your own?"

His question fully answered, the devotee thanked Chan Master Wúxiāng and left.

Everyone has their own personal vows. That is why it is unnecessary to ask others about their vows. First of all, what you would like to do for sentient beings? Vows can be great or small. One can vow to become a cow who nourishes or a tree that shelters. We can also vow to achieve sagehood or buddhahood. With the impetus generated by the vow, we will be able to bear pain and overcome hardships. If one is willing to labor for the sake of sentient beings, then one will be able to achieve this vow. So long as a vow is not falsely pledged, it will surely succeed.

Only with resolve do we have the power to consummate our ideals and vows. Vows are the origin of all successful endeavors.

Personal Commitment

Chan Master Yángqí Fānghuì was quite intelligent and sharp-witted in his youth. He became a monk on Mount Dàowú in Tánzhōu, Húnán and studied Buddhist *sutras*. It was said that he remembered perfectly the *sutras* that he'd read. He studied under Chan Master Shíshuāng Chǔyuán for a long period of time, and volunteered to serve as the superintendent of Chan Master Chǔyuán's temple.

Although he spent ten years there, he had never been able to attain enlightenment. Every time he went to Chan Master Chǔyuán for instruction, the master would reply, "Your work is so arduous. Let's talk later!"

One day, he went to ask Chan Master Chǔyuán for instruction. The older monk said, "Superintendent, your future generations of disciples will fill the world and be prosperous. Yet you are anxious to realize the Way. What's your hurry?"

On another day, Chan Master Chǔyuán left the temple and it suddenly began to rain. Chan Master Fānghuì was waiting for him on the side of a small road. As soon as he saw Chan Master Chǔyuán, he immediately brought him over and said, "Master, today you must give me instruction or I won't let you go back to the temple."

Chan Master Chǔyuán replied, "Superintendent! If you want to know about this matter, then rest all things!"

Right after he finished speaking, Chan Master Fānghuì's ears boomed with his master's words and a light flashed through his mind. In that instant, he experienced great enlightenment. He prostrated before his master on the rain soaked ground, sweat, tears, and rain flowing together. He cried out, "Now I have rested all things. Now I have rested all things!"

One day, Chan Master Chǔyuán entered the Dharma hall to deliver a talk. Chan Master Fānghuì addressed the audience, "How is the moment, when hidden birds twitter about, leaving the clouds behind and enter into uneven mountain peaks?"

Chan Master Chǔyuán replied, "I walk through wild grasses, while you again enter deeply into the village!"

Chan Master Fānghuì spoke again: "Though all things have rested, I further ask once more."

Chan Master Chǔyuán gave a powerful shout.

Chan Master Fānghuì praised, "Good shout!"

Chan Master Chǔyuán shouted again.

Chan Master Fānghuì joined him in the shouting.

Chan Master Chǔyuán followed this with two consecutive shouts.

Chan Master Fānghuì prostrated before him.

After Chan Master Fānghuì finished his homage, with reverence and sincerity he said, "Master, this matter must be shouldered by oneself!"

After Chan Master Chǔyuán heard this, he brushed off his sleeves and walked away.

Chan Master Chǔyuán refused to rush into complete verbal instruction for Chan Master Fānghuì. Chan Master Chǔyuán hoped that Fānghuì would first cultivate himself and wait for favorable circumstances. However, Chan Master Fānghuì was too eager to gain enlightenment, so he had to say it. Later, Fānghuì said "Now I have rested all things," and further remarked that there must be personal commitments for all things. Chan Master Chǔyuán brushed his sleeves to indicate it was now Chan Master Fānghuì's responsibility. Chan Master Fānghuì later spoke this gatha, "The mind follows the myriad states as they revolve and change. The turning point can be deep and hidden. Following the flow to recognize ones nature. There exists neither joy nor sorrow." He had already gained true entry into the state of Chan.

Has He Ever Spoken to You?

During the Tang dynasty, there was a Chan Master Cuìwēi Wúxué. The details of his life are unknown, but he was the Dharma heir of Chan Master Dānxiá Tiānrán. After he received the Dharma from Chan Master Dānxiá Tiānrán, he moved to serve as the abbot of Cuìwēi Temple on Mount Zhōngnán in the Jīngzhào prefecture (present day Cháng'ān region).

One day, when Chan Master Wúxué was offering incense to an icon of an arhat inside the Buddha Hall. A student monk saw this and was puzzled, so asked, "Chan Master, our patriarch Dānxiá Tiānrán taught that in Chan we should not become attached to external forms, so even wooden icons of Buddha can be burned like firewood. We do this to eradicate the defilement of self-attachment of sentient beings. Furthermore, the rank of arhat is less than that of a buddha. Why do you offer incense to this arhat icon?"

Chan Master Wúxué paid him no heed. He quietly offered the incense stick, made a bow, and placed the incense into the cauldron. Lifting his head to the arhat, he said, "It cannot be burnt. Let those who wish to make offerings be left alone to make offerings."

The student monk persisted, "Master, every day you offer incense offerings to this arhat. Has he ever spoken to you?"

Chan Master Wúxué suddenly turned to face the student monk and asked back, "Let me ask you; you eat every day, don't you?"

The student monk was surprised and uncertain how to answer.

Chan Master Wúxué then scolded him saying, "Chan is natural and spontaneous. There is no need to differentiate and conceptualize. Whether it is burning wooden icons of Buddha or making offerings to arhats; whether an arhat speaks any words to me or comes to me, that is all up to him. You should just go eat your meals. Why bother yourself over all these trivial matters?"

The student monk heard these words and experienced a slight awakening.

Chan Master Dānxiá Tiānrán was originally a scholar. He intended to attend the imperial exams and earn a government position. However, a Chan master told him, "rather than become an official, seek to become a buddha." Moved by these words, he brought a basin of water to his mentor and requested that his mentor shave his head to become a monk. Later in life he became known for burning a statue of a buddha as firewood in order to eradicate people's attachment to forms. Hence, the story of "Danxia burning buddha."

Buddhist icons are meant to be venerated and should not be burned casually. Chan Master Dānxiá Tiānrán was able to burn buddha statues because he had already realized that his own mind is buddha. The young student monk had not yet attained that level of understanding. Consequently, Chan Master Wúxué instructed him to just go eat your meals, to take care of his own mind and not bother himself with other people's business!

Twice Over Gōng'Àns

Monk Běi Chánjì, also known as Chan Master Wùtōng, was a native of Qízhōu (present day Qíchūn, Húběi). He received the Dharma from Chan Master Yúnmén Wényǎn during the time of the late Tang dynasty and Five Dynasties period.

One day, a monk came to Bei Chan Monastery to pay respects to Monk Běi Chánjì; he asked, "Where are you from?"

The monk respectfully replied, "This student monk comes from Huángzhōu (present day Huánggǎng area in Húběi)."

Monk Běi Chánjì continued, "Which temple did you live in?"

The monk responded, "This student monk lived in Zīfú (resource and merit) Monastery."

Hearing this, Monk Běi Chánjì asked, "Given that you're from Zīfú Monastery, your resource and merit are sure to be quite considerable, right?"

The monk answered, "Not much, 'twice over gōng'àn' are not worth discussing."

Monk Běi Chánjì looked at the monk and asked, "Since you traveled from Zīfú Monastery, you still need to explain somewhat!"

The monk replied, "One was 'facing a thousand miles' and the second one was 'the walls have ears.' How am I supposed to talk?"

Monk Běi Chánjì was now sure that this visitor wasan expert in Chan. He instructed the guest hall to provide a good reception for the monk.

In Chan Buddhism, "twice over gōng'àn" means those people who are only capable of mimicking the gōng'àn responses of others. They may use or comment on them, striking a pose. However, they could not surpass the meaning of what was said by the virtuous ones before them because these are just unnecessary add-ons. Therefore, some Chan practitioners echo the views of others, not coming up with any new meaning. These are merely twice over gōng'àns.

During their interaction, the student monk wanted Monk Běi Chánjì to realize that he was not a simple mimic, twice over gōng'àns practitioner. So in saying "facing a thousand miles" means how can one hear from a thousand miles away? Then he went on to say "the walls have ears," when there are ears around to listen how is one supposed to speak? In other words, in asking about the student monk's accumulated virtue, people who came before had already spoken of it, and therefore, I need not speak anymore. That is why in Chan Buddhism, as soon as you speak, others will know whether you got it or not.

Thirty More Lashes

One day, all the monks in the monastery went for chores, Chan Master Wéishān Língyòu and his disciple, Chan Master Yǎngshān Huìjì followed the group up the mountain to pick tea leaves.

Chan Master Wéishān asked Chan Master Yǎngshān, "How is it that while picking tea leaves all day long, I have only heard your voice but I have not seen your physical body?"

Immediately upon hearing that, Chan Master Yǎngshān shook the tea tree to demonstrate his realization of Chan.

Chan Master Wéishān did not accept Chan Master Yǎngshān's action and commented, "You only understand its function, but not attain its essence."

Chan Master Yǎngshān did not admit the criticism and countered, "Master, so what is your state?"

Chan Master Wéishān fell silent, not saying a word.

After observing his master's silence for some time, Chan Master Yǎngshān challenged him by saying, "Only gain its essence, but not its function."

Chan Master Wéishān responded instantly with, "I'm going to give you thirty lashes!"

Chan Master Yǎngshān immediately countered, "My master's discipline rod strikes me, but who should my discipline rod strike?"

Chan Master Wéishān instantly replied, "Thirty more lashes for you!"

Chan Master Yǎngshān shook the tea tree to demonstrate the marvelous function of Chan. Chan Master Wéishān fell into a speechless silence to show that the original essence of Chan is formless and not to be described with spoken words. However, Master Yǎngshān insisted on speaking, and he naturally had to take thirty lashes for having done so.

Chan Master Yǎngshān figured since his master pointed out that he had "function" but lacked "essence," what would be the harm in pointing out that his master had "essence" but lacked "function?" If what his master said was wrong, then his master should also receive lashes as a punishment, right? He thereby implied it by asking his master, "My master's discipline rod will strike me, but who should my discipline rod strike?" Of course, there was no avoiding another thirty lashes. Little did he know that speaking about "function" was harmless, but as soon as he spoke about something ineffable such as "essence" which transcends movement and stillness, it was wrong. Because essence is as such, if you give rise to thought, it will be contradictory.

In Chan Buddhism, masters and disciples challenge one another back and forth in their sharp debates. Sometimes they exhibit lively wittiness, are harsh and stern, skillfully draw upon personal warmth, and sometimes "attaining the Way will result in thirty lashes and failure to attain the Way will likewise result in thirty lashes." No matter how these interactions play out, they all contain the masters' deep compassion and a loving concern for their disciples.

Mutually Related

Chan Master Yúnyán Tánchéng was a native of Jiāngxī during the Tang dynasty. He became a monk in his youth and studied under the tutelage of Chan Master Bǎizhàng Huáihǎi. After Chan Master Bǎizhàng Huáihǎi passed away, he went to Lǐzhōu (present day Lǐ county) in Húnán to study under Chan Master Yàoshān Wéiyǎn and later inherited the Dharma lineage.

One day, Venerable Yúnyán was working in the vegetable garden when Chan Master Yàoshān Wéiyǎn happened to pass by and asked, "What are you doing?"

Venerable Yúnyán stopped working and answered, "He is carrying a load of manure, Master." In answering like this, Venerable Yúnyán was referring to himself as a putrid sack.

Chan Master Yàoshān Wéiyǎn walked over to Venerable Yúnyán, stood by his side, and whispered, "Is that person still here?"

Venerable Yúnyán knew that Chan Master Yàoshān Wéiyǎn was testing him so he followed along with the *huàtóu*, and whispered back into his ear, "He's still here!" This answer meant that there had been no progress.

Chan Master Yàoshān Wéiyǎn asked him once more, "For whom is it that you are ultimately performing all of this coming and going?"

Venerable Yúnyán swung his hands and said, "It is not for anyone. I am just running around on his behalf, that's all!"

Chan Master Yàoshān Wéiyǎn then said, "Since that's how it is, why don't you have him accompany you on your way?"

That very moment, Venerable Yúnyán finally understood the meaning behind his words, unruffled he replied, "With regards to walking and carrying a load, aren't they mutually related?"

Chan Master Yàoshān Wéiyǎn nodded approvingly and remarked, "Indeed, indeed."

As Chan Master Yàoshān Wéiyǎn walked away he turned back and added, "You treat him well!"

No matter what people do, they often shift the blame onto others for mistakes while taking the credit for themselves. But if one instead credited others for their work, their ability would increase. In this world, we often compare ourselves to others, comparing who has more and less, differentiating between who is busier or who is more idle, who has more or less merits. But if we were able to visualize ourselves as the putrid sack as Chan Master Yúnyán did, we would be able to bear great loads. Chan Master Yàoshān Wéiyǎn had already mastered the understanding of the non-dual nature of self and other. That is why he was able to encourage Chan Master Yúnyán by saying, "You treat him well!"

The Buddha Hall has No Buddha

When Chan Master Fénzhōu Wúyè from Shānxī first met Chan Master Mǎzǔ Dàoyī, due to his imposing physique and a voice loud as a large bell, Chan Master Mǎzǔ teased him by remarking, "What a majestic Buddha Hall, but inside there is no buddha!"

Venerable Wúyè immediately bowed and then respectfully spoke: "With regards to the teachings of the *Three Vehicles*, I am confident that I have at least some crude understanding of their principles. However, the Chan School states that this mind is buddha. I haven't truly comprehended this teaching yet."

Chan Master Mǎzǔ could see his sincerity and instructed, "You have yet to comprehend the mind that 'is as is,' there is nothing other than that. When one does not comprehend, it is ignorance; if realized, it is enlightenment. Ignorance is sentient beings, enlightenment is buddha."

Wúyè asked further, "Is there any Dharma outside of the mind, buddha, and sentient beings?"

Mǎzǔ answered, "There is no difference between the mind, buddha, and sentient beings. How could there be any other Dharma? Like a hand can be balled up into a fist, when the fist is unfolded it is a hand."

Wúyè then asked, "What is the intent of the Patriarch Coming from the West?"

Mǎzǔ answered, "Where is the Patriarch now? You should take your leave. Come back again some other time."

Chan Master Wúyè had no recourse but to bid farewell and as he was stepping over the doorsill, Mǎzǔ shouted "Virtuous one!" Chan Master Wúyè promptly looked back.

Măzŭ asked, "What is it?"

Chan Master Wúyè immediately dropped to his knees to pay homage. Tearfully, he said, "It was said the path to buddhahood is long, but only now have I understood. The true form of the Dharmakāya is fundamentally and naturally intrinsic."

At this point, Chan Master Măzŭ finally offered praise, remarking, "This dummy has awakened!"

Speaking of cultivation, sometimes it is asked how much time it takes to achieve Buddhahood. If we say that Buddhahood is distant, then it would require three great kalpas. If we say that Buddhahood is near, then it is right here and now. Chan Master Dàjué Huáiliǎn once said, "In the buddha halls of old it was never said any differently. It flows from within a sentence, and there has been much discussion regarding it." When we seek Dharma from outside of our mind and lose ourselves, we become a burden to the Buddha and enlightened masters. Only after being told thousands of times, do we finally know to turn back. As soon as Măzŭ spoke, Wúyè turned back, and in the here and now he recognized his original face. "Fish in water should stop searching for water, and those who journey a day amid the mountain ridges should stop seeking for mountains." You could say that Wúyè was a dummy, but once a Chan mind is awakened, one can realize self.

Where is the True Buddha?

Chan Master Nántǎ Guāngyǒng was a monk during the Later Tang dynasty of the Five Dynasties period. His secular family name was Zhāng and a native of Fēngchéng, Jiāngxī. It was said that he was named "Guāngyǒng (welling up with light)" because of the divine light which shined upon the doorway at the time of his birth. Even as a youth, he displayed extraordinary intelligence. Later on, he studied under Chan Master Yǎngshān Huìjì, and during this period, Chan Master Yǎngshān often praised him as "a buddha in the flesh." After he inherited the Dharma from Chan Master Yǎngshān Huìjì, he went to Nántǎ, Yǎngshān to teach the Dharma.

One day, a student monk asked Chan Master Guāngyǒng, "Mañjuśrī was a teacher to the seven buddhas of the past. May I please ask: did Mañjuśrī Bodhisattva also have a teacher?"

Chan Master Guāngyǒng replied, "When conditions are there; there'd be one."

The student monk continued, "Then who was Mañjuśrī Bodhisattva's teacher?"

Without speaking a word, Chan Master Guāngyǒng lifted the duster in his hand and showed him.

The student monk said, "This is it?"

At that time, Chan Master Guāngyǒng put the duster down and then folded his arms before his chest.

The student monk continued, "Chan Master, please say something."

Chan Master Guāngyŏng slowly uttered, "When water flows; there'd be a canal."

The student monk asked, "Then may I please ask: where is the true buddha?"

Chan Master Guāngyŏng solemnly replied, "The true buddha you speak of is none other than yourself. It is unfortunate that you do not recognize it!"

The student monk asked again, "Then how should I go about recognizing that?"

Chan Master Guāngyŏng replied, "You would never dare to shoulder the responsibility. What use is there in telling you?"

The student monk said doubtfully, "Could it be that if I dared to shoulder the responsibility, then I would be a buddha?"

Chan Master Guāngyŏng nodded and replied seriously, "If you 'practice as a buddha,' then of course you are a buddha!"

People always forget that their own minds are buddha, that their original nature is buddha. They seek buddha outside of themselves. Praying to the Buddha, paying homage to the Buddha, and reciting the Buddha's name they only have faith in the Buddha, but they do not recognize themselves as a buddha. If, for instance, one is willing to admit and shoulder the responsibility that "I am buddha," then one will practice like the Buddha and do what the Buddha would do; no longer give rise to greed and anger and no longer entertain worldly desires, give kindness and to spread joy to the world, then how would one not be a buddha?

You Have Yet to Awaken

During the Song dynasty, Chan Master Dàhuì Zōnggǎo from the Línjì School served as the head monk at his temple on Mount Yúnjū. One day, he went to Xījī Village to run an errand. A young monk learned of this and made a special trip there to request Dharma instruction from the Chan Master. The monk joined his palms together and greeted Chan Master Dàhuì with a bow. He respectfully spoke, "In the past I heard you discuss the Chan story 'a girl exits meditative concentration,' and I believe I attained some degree of enlightenment. I have come here to ask you to verify this for me, Chan Master."

The Chan *gōng'àn* of "a girl exits meditative concentration" is a reference to an incident that occurred during one of the Buddha's Dharma talks, when a girl sitting next to the Buddha entered into meditative concentration. Mañjuśrī Bodhisattva asked the Buddha how a girl was able to enter into meditative concentration while Mañjuśrī himself was still unable to do so.

The Buddha wanted Mañjuśrī Bodhisattva to bring her out of meditative concentration so that Mañjuśrī Bodhisattva could ask her directly. Mañjuśrī Bodhisattva circumambulated the girl three times and snapped his fingers, but the girl was immoveable. The Buddha said that even hundreds of thousands of Mañjuśrīs would all fail at this task and that only Jālinīprabha Bodhisattva would be able to succeed. Just as expected, Jālinīprabha Bodhisattva came before the girl and with a snap of his fingers, the girl immediately exited meditative concentration.

Chan Master Dàhuì heard the wandering monk's request, and immediately scolded him. "Get out of here! You haven't awakened yet."

The monk was shocked, but he continued his line of questioning, "Chan Master, I haven't finished what I am saying. Why do you say I haven't awakened yet?"

Chan Master Dàhuì waved him off and repeated, "Get out of here! You haven't awakened yet." And with that, he turned to walk away.

The wandering monk looked at Chan Master Dàhuì's silhouette and finally understood: if the necessary causes and conditions are insufficient, then even countless words of explanation would not be of any use.

After Chan Master Dàhuì Zōnggǎo proclaimed that the monk had yet to awaken, the Chan Master left. As this monk saw the Chan Master's silhouette he thought to himself, "The causes and conditions have not been met. Nothing can be done about that." This monk was truly an insightful individual.

All phenomena within the world arise from dependent origination, and in this case, the requisite causes and conditions were incomplete. Even if the monk was enlightened, with no one to verify it, he still could not "graduate." Consequently, the student monk was only able to lament that the causes and conditions of his meritorious virtues were inadequate. He did not even blame Chan Master Dàhuì Zōnggǎo for being less than courteous with him. A true Chan practitioner is able to think positively and doing so is a form of insight. For those with insight, do they have to worry about not gaining enlightenment?

No Mind is the Way

Someone once asked Chan Master Sīkōng Běnjìng, "What is the Way?" Chan Master Sīkōng Běnjìng answered, "No Mind is the Way."

Regarding this, Chan Master Zhěn put forth the question, "Since the Way has no mind, so did the Buddha have a mind? Might I please ask: are buddha and the Way the same or are they two separate matters?"

Chan Master Sīkōng Běnjìng replied, "A buddha and the Way are neither the same nor different."

Chan Master Zhěn asked further, "Buddhas have minds and are able to liberate sentient beings. The Way has no mind and is unable liberate sentient beings. Among these two, one can liberate sentient beings, and the other does not liberate sentient beings. How can it be said that there is no difference between them?"

Master Sīkōng Běnjìng then went a step further in his explanation saying, "If you say that buddhas liberate sentient beings and the Way does not, then you are giving rise to deluded duality. In actuality, "buddha" is just a name and the Way is likewise an arbitrary construct. Both "Buddha" and "the Way" are not real; they are nominal designations. Given that they are both nominal designations, why still distinguish one from the other."

Chan Master Zhěn was still confused and asked, "If 'buddha' and 'the Way' are both nominal designations, then who established these nominal designations? Given that they have already been established, how can one say they don't exist?"

Chan Master Sīkōng Běnjìng responded saying, "Buddha and the Way are established by the mind. If one investigates that mind which established them, one actually discovers that there is no mind. Since the mind does not exist, then awakening to "buddha" and "the Way" is not real. Since one then knows that they are like dreams and illusions, then one immediately awakens to 'it is intrinsically empty.' If one forcibly expresses the nominal constructs of 'buddhas' and 'the Way,' then this is just the understanding of practitioners of the Two Vehicles."

Lastly, Chan Master Sīkōng Běnjìng recited the *Gāthā of No Cultivation and No Practice*:

"Seeing the Way, one begins cultivation. Not seeing it; why cultivate? The nature of the Way is like space, how can space be cultivated? Observe all cultivators of the Way, stirring fire in search for bubbles. Like watching puppetry, when the strings are cut, all come to cease."

"No mind" is the mind which does not give rise to attachments. If we have "no mind" in our daily lives, then we will not differentiate based on attraction and aversion when encountering external conditions. Then we will be able to attain ease in all conditions, and not become obstructed by attachment and clinging. Many people spend all day engrossed in dealings for fame, fortune, and power and the gains and losses in love and relationships. How could they ever have peace and ease from no mind in following conditions? If people are able to have no cravings, then they will have no preoccupation in their minds, with no craving and preoccupation in the mind; that is liberation.

Ancient Stream, Cold Spring

Chan Master Xuěfēng Yìcún from the Tang dynasty, whose secular family name was Zēng, was a native of Quánzhōu, Fújiàn. At age seventeen, he became a monk; several years later, he went to Bǎochà Temple in Yōuzhōu, Héběi to receive full ordination. After that, he studied in different monasteries, most notably under Chan Master Déshān Xuānjiàn from Wǔlíng, Húnán province. He further received the essence of the Dharma from Chan Master Déshān Xuānjiàn. Later in life, he founded a temple on Mount Xiànggǔ in Fúzhōu, where he taught the Dharma. Due to the year end seasonal coldness on Mount Xiànggǔ where it often snowed before winter arrived, Chan Master Yìcún took "Xuěfēng (Snow-Capped Peaks)" as his Dharma name.

When Chan Master Xuěfēng Yìcún guided students, he often used sharp-edged rhetoric and cryptic language to make his points understood by the student monks, never falling into the entrapment of textual language. For example, if monks took the initiative to ask about a given doubt, he would turn the question around on the questioners to impel them to find their own paths.

One day, a young monk asked Chan Master Xuěfēng Yìcún, "Chan Master, what does 'ancient stream, cold spring' mean?"

Chan Master Xuěfēng Yìcún yelled, "The Chan mind is unpredictable!"

The monk heard these words and frowned in confusion. He asked once more, "However, shouldn't you give an explanation?"

Chan Master Xuěfēng Yìcún smiled faintly and replied, "Well, that is up to you to explore on your own."

The mind of each person is like "enduring emptiness of the universe since ancient times," intrinsic pure self-nature. When states arise from the sensory roots encountering external dusts, they are like "shifting wind and changing moon in one day" within the enduring emptiness of the universe since ancient times. While various winds, moon, clouds, and rains come and go within the enduring emptiness, the enduring emptiness has always been as such, unaffected by the changes.

Covering the Body Shell

Little is known about the life of Chan Master Jiāngxī Bēishù. He was a Dharma heir of Chan Master Mǎzǔ Dàoyī of the Tang dynasty.

One day, Chan Master Jiāngxī Bēishù laid down on the ground to rest from the scorching weather. Seeing this, Chan Master Dàowú brought over a blanket and covered him with it.

Chan Master Jiāngxī Bēishù was startled by Chan Master Dàowú's sudden action. Wide eyed, he asked, "What are doing?"

Chan Master Dàowú smiled faintly and replied, "I wanted to cover this shell of your body."

Chan Master Jiāngxī Bēishù carefully contemplated these words. Finally, he calmly said, "You said that you would like to cover this shell of a body. May I please ask, would it be better for this shell to be seated or lying?"

Chan Master Dàowú playfully responded, "To me, neither is good."

Chan Master Jiāngxī Bēishù suddenly sprung up to his feet and ripped off the blanket shouting, "Then what are you covering in the first place?"

Chan Master Dàowú then said, "You don't care whether you are sitting or lying, so why would you care about a cover?"

Chan Master Jiāngxī Bēishù replied, "I don't care whether I sit or lie; so I don't even want a cover."

Chan Master Dàowú laughed and walked away not looking back.

These two monks are both regarded as accomplished practitioners of the Chan School. They were considered on par with each other, and tested each other's attainments in daily life. Chan Master Jiāngxī Bēishù believed himself to already be free and liberated and Chan Master Dàowú believed that he still needed to be looked after. However, looking after someone is not simply a matter of covering them with a blanket!

Someone who does not care whether it is sitting or lying, does not want a cover, has no possessions, and has let go of everything. Isn't that freedom and ease in the here and now? After Chan Master Dàowú came to understand the mind of his equal, he exited with a laugh.

Is it not fascinating how these two Chan practitioners tested each other's efficacy?

Borrowed by Someone Else

There were two student monks who lived in separate thatched huts. One lived in a hut up high and the other lived in a hut down low. They had not seen each other for many days.

One day, the two met one another, and the monk from the higher hut said to the monk from the lower hut, "I haven't seen you in many days. What have you been busy with?"

The student monk from the lower hut replied, "I've been busy constructing a seamless pagoda."

The monk from the higher hut was delighted to hear that. He said, "I had just been thinking about making a seamless pagoda. Could I borrow your seamless pagoda and use its design as my reference?"

The monk from the lower hut answered, "How unfortunate. I wish you had said something earlier. Someone else has borrowed my seamless pagoda."

The monk from the higher hut confidently offered, "That's okay. Just use your own form, what you have, the one that is not fixed. Can you show me that seamless pagoda?"

A seamless pagoda is the Dharma body of our original nature. The Dharma body of the original nature of all sentient beings is a truly seamless pagoda. It permeates emptiness, swelling through the Dharma Realm. What else could be called a seamless pagoda, if not the fulfilled

Dharma body? The Dharma body is timeless and unchanging. It has been perpetual throughout the incalculable kalpas. Do not focus on the bodily forms it inhabits. Everyone has Buddha nature and Dharma body. There are even cases where after cremation, the body remains undamaged. Those are relics of the Dharma body.

It was through this Dharma nature that the Buddha attained enlightenment. All that the Buddha taught in the sutras can also be called the Dharma body. In the Diamond Sūtra it says, "Wherever there is this sūtra, the offerings made by devas, humans and asuras will be as if they were made in a pagoda." Sutras are seamless pagodas. The student monk from the lower hut had an understanding of the limitless Dharma body and so knew to build a seamless pagoda to offer to the Dharma body; to realize the Dharma body.

The monk from the lower hut claimed that his own seamless pagoda had been borrowed by someone else. However, the original nature of the Dharma body cannot be borrowed. It was through realizing this that the monk from the higher hut came to understand the truth.

What do You Fear?

During the Tang dynasty, there was a Chan master, Lóngshòu Shàoqīng from Zhāngzhōu (present day Fújiàn) who was a Dharma heir to Chan Master Xuěfēng Yìcún. He became a monk as a child and excelled in various scholastic studies. Later in life, he came to study at the temple of Chan Master Xuěfēng Yìcún and served as his attendant for quite a number of years.

One day, Chan Master Lóngshòu Shàoqīng was accompanying Chan Master Xuěfēng Yìcún during a walking meditation on a mountain. Suddenly, strong gusts began which caused the wild yams next to the path to start blowing around incessantly.

Chan Master Xuěfēng Yìcún saw this, and pointed to the yam leaves being blown back and forth. He turned his head to Chan Master Lóngshòu Shàoqīng and said, "Look over here!"

He saw that Chan Master Lóngshòu Shàoqīng looked panic-stricken, and he exclaimed, "Master, I'm frightened!"

Chan Master Xuěfēng Yìcún pointedly asked in response, "This is something from your own household. What is exactly that you fear?"

Hearing this, Chan Master Lóngshòu Shàoqīng achieved great awakening in that moment. Not long after that incident, he received an invitation to expound the Dharma in Lóngxī.

Chan Master Lóngshòu Shàoqīng was not actually afraid of the wild yams blowing in the wind, but instead this was alluding to the fear of the karmic winds of ignorance which blow sentient beings into negative rebirths of saṃsāra. However, Chan Master Xuěfēng Yìcún was able to explain the teachings for Chan Master Lóngshòu Shàoqīng, saying, "This is something from your own household," means ignorance and enlightenment both originate in our minds and do not come from some external source. Although our minds give rise to confusion and create karma and also propel our births and deaths throughout saṃsāra, they also transform worries into wisdom and the attainment of Buddhahood.

The saying "worry is bodhi" means that without worries, there is no wisdom to be gained. It takes but one thought to transform ignorance into enlightenment and malevolence into benevolence. Given that, what is there to fear? If each day we can focus our minds, stay present, maintain sincerity, act with virtue, and shed desires and greed, then what worries would we have regarding our capacity to treat the fear and ignorance within our minds?

I am Liángsuì

During the Tang dynasty Chan Master Shòuzhōu Liángsuì from the Nányuè Huáiràng Dharma lineage was a disciple of Chan Master Mágǔ Bǎochè from whom he received Dharma transmission. When he had just arrived to visit Chan Master Bǎochè at Mount Mágǔ in Shānxī, the Chan Master said nothing to him but instead picked up a hoe and started walking towards the garden where he would be weeding. Shòuzhōu Liángsuì saw this and followed Chan Master Bǎochè closely from behind all the way to the garden, but the Chan Master did not so much as acknowledge his presence.

After Chan Master Bǎochè finished weeding, he returned to the abbot's quarters and coldly closed the door behind. The meeting that Shòuzhōu Liángsuì had hoped for was not only unsuccessful, he was also ignored. There was nothing to do except go back to the itinerant monastics quarters.

Bright and early the next morning, Shòuzhōu Liángsuì went again to visit the monk, but the door to the abbot's quarters was still closed tightly, so he knocked and knocked on the door. From within the abbot's quarters, Chan Master Bǎochè loudly asked, "Who's outside my door?"

Liángsuì answered back, "Liángsuì!" At that very moment, it was as though lightning flashed through his mind. The ignorance shattered as he achieved sudden awakening. Liángsuì followed up in a loud voice, "Great Monk, thank you for calling 'Liángsuì' back. In the past I had been deceived by *sutras* and commentaries. I had no idea what my original face looked like until today. Thank you, benevolent teacher. Liángsuì bows before you now."

At that time, Chan Master Bǎochè finally opened the door to meet Liángsuì and took him to the Dharma hall. Chan Master Bǎochè pointed at Shòuzhōu Liángsuì and told the assembled monastics, "Liángsuì knows everything that you do, but what Liángsuì knows is something you do not."

A Chan practitioner must read a thousand sutras and commentaries, understand the various wisdom within a thousand different principles and concepts in order to realize non-differentiating wisdom for realizing the Way. Therefore, Chan practitioners could not attain enlightenment without reading and studying sutras and commentaries. The Sixth Patriarch Huineng, on hearing the Nirvana Sutra *from Wujinzang Bhiksuni, was able to explain the sutra to her. In the* Platform Sutra: *Chan Master Fahai from Shaozhou came to discuss "the mind is the buddha," Venerable Fada from Hongzhou came to discuss the essence of the* Lotus Sutra, *Venerable Zhitong from Shouzhou came to discuss the meaning of "Mind-only," and Chan Master Sengzhi from Xinzhou came to discuss "perspectives of the tathagata" etc... So it is clear that the Sixth Patriarch was not illiterate, nor lacking in understanding of the sutras.*

When Chan Master Bǎochè asked Chan Master Liángsuì who was outside his door, he answered, "Liángsuì" and then achieved sudden awakening. Although Chan Master Liángsuì said that in the past he had been deceived by sutras and commentaries, those sutras and commentaries had fostered his awakening. Consequently, Chan Master Bǎochè brought Chan Master Liángsuì to meet the assembled monks in the Dharma hall. In addition, he confirmed Chan Master Liángsuì's experience by announcing, "Liángsuì knows everything that you do, while none of you know what Liángsuì knows."

To Have Almost Spent a Life in Vain

Chan Master Jīnjué Wùchè's school had over one thousand three hundred monks. These monks spread themselves all over China to spread the Dharma, benefit beings, and serve people. Among Chan Master Jīnjué's disciples was a Chan monk known as Cōnghuì. He had studied under Chan Master Jīnjué's guidance for many years and diligently engaged in practicing the Dharma with the rest of the community. Despite these efforts, he had never been able to know.

One day, Cōnghuì went to visit Chan Master Jīnjué Wùchè. Wanting to test out his student's capacity, Chan Master Jīnjué shouted his name: "Cōnghuì!"

Cōnghuì respectfully answered, "Your student is here."

As if he hadn't heard him, Chan Master Jīnjué called out again, "Cōnghuì!"

Cōng Huì replied, "Your student is here!"

Chan Master Jīnjué called his name out once more: "Cōnghuì!"

Cōnghuì still affirmed, "Your student is here!"

Three times he was called, and three times Cōnghuì answered, "Your student is here."

Chan Master Jīnjué could not help but reproach his student: "You are such a dull monk; don't complain that I failed you when you look back on this!"

After being scolded, Cōnghuì suddenly had a realization. He happily remarked, "Master, don't scold me first.

If Cōnghuì, had not come to pay his respects to you today, I fear I would have spent my life in vain."

At this time, Chan Master Jīnjué Wùchè nodded, approving Cōnghuì's answer.

Chan emphasizes both capacity and functionality. In order to attain enlightenment, one needs the appropriate causes and conditions, like threading a needle that leads to one's opportunity. Chan Master Jīnjué Wùchè called out Cōnghuì's name three times. Cōnghuì replied each time. There was nothing wrong with his reaction, but it is merely the appropriate reaction according to the mannerisms of the mundane world. Naturally, Chan Master Jīnjué was not satisfied by this answer. In an effort to help his student, he yelled at Cōnghuì: "You are such a dull monk!" The message was that Chan Master Cōnghuì was acting unbearably mundane and that this was not a situation that called for mundane ceremonial politeness. One cannot enter the Way in this manner.

After hearing Chan Master Jīnjué Wùchè's harsh reproach, Cōnghuì finally gained some degree of enlightenment. This was why he quickly replied that if he had not received his master's guidance, he would have lived his life in vain.

Chan Master Jīnjué heard this answer and knew that Cōnghuì had come to understand the meaning of Chan. They were now of the same mind. Later, Chan Master Jīnjué Wùchè would transmit his Chan Dharma to him.

The Mind and the Way

are of a Singular Suchness

One day, Chan Master Yuǎn came to Mount Sīkōng to ask Chan Master Běnjìng, "Master, may I please ask: according to your own viewpoint, what is the Way?"

Chan Master Sīkōng Běnjìng answered, "No-mind is the Way."

Chan Master Yuǎn inquired further, "The Way originates in the mind. How can you say that no-mind is the Way?"

"The Way originally has no name. It is the mind that labels it as "the Way." Once labeled "the Way," it is no longer empty. If the mind itself is ultimately also empty, then does the Way really originate from the mind? Both are ultimately empty, false labels we place on terms."

Chan Master Yuǎn continued elaborating, "Is the body-mind that you have now a form of the Way?"

With great certainty, Chan Master Sīkōng Běnjìng answered, "Of course this mountain monk's body-mind is of the Way!"

Chan Master Yuǎn asked back, "Chan Master, you just said that no-mind is the Way. But now you are saying that your body-mind is the Way. Is this not a contradiction?"

Chan Master Sīkōng Běnjìng laughed in response, "No-mind is the Way. When the mind dissipates, the Way reverts to emptiness. The Way and the mind are one. That is why I say that no-mind is the Way. Furthermore, the body-mind is the Way, just as the Way is the body-mind.

The body-mind is originally empty. Thus, the Way is empty."

Chan Master Yuǎn quipped, "Master, you seem so small and frail, yet you are able to awaken to such a truth."

Chan Master Sīkōng Běnjìng replied, "Praiseworthy one, you only see the form of this mountain monk, but you fail to see my non-form. The form is what one sees with their eyes. Is it stated in the *sutras* that ordinary forms are all illusory. If you are able to see all forms are not real, then you will awaken to this truth. But if you take forms to be real, you will never awaken to the Way!"

When Chan Master Sīkōng Běnjìng instructed, he stressed that "this mind is Buddha, no-mind is the Way" as the core of his teachings and the entry point into the gates of Dharma. The Buddha is in the mind; the Way is in the present moment. No-mind is the absence of mundane thoughts, ideas, and desires. Chan Master Yuǎn did not understand what Chan Master Sīkōng Běnjìng meant when he stated that "no-mind is the Way." He was attached to the delusion that his body-mind either was or was not the Way. His mentor explained to him that "forms are all illusory. If you are able to see all forms are not forms, then you will awaken to the truth."

Chan is one's original, natural face. All matters can be met without the deliberate use of the mind. This is because using the mind gives rise to form. The Dharma of non-existence and the Chan mind are interdependent.

Emptiness and Form are Originally the Same

One day, a student monk came to Chan Master Zhàozhōu Cóngshěn for instructions. He asked, "How can one explain the principle of 'form is emptiness and emptiness is form?'"

Chan Master Zhàozhōu Cóngshěn replied with the verse, "Obstructions are not walls, no empty space within passages; if one understands this, then emptiness and form are the same."

The student monk did not understand. Chan Master Zhàozhōu continued:

"Buddha nature is plain to see, but it is difficult for sentient beings with attachments to see it. If one is awakened to the truth of sentient beings have no-self, then my face is the Buddha's face."

Still perplexed, the student monk asked, "Chan Master, I asked you how 'form is emptiness and emptiness is form.' Why did you respond to me with this *gatha*?"

Chan Master Zhàozhōu gave a stare with his eyes and answered, "Form is emptiness; emptiness is form!" At these words, the student monk awakened.

In Buddhism, all the material things in the world are called form. They rely upon causes and conditions to come into being and cannot exist independently. Therefore, there is no inherent nature to attain. With nothing to attain, they are "empty." Thus, form's nature is empty. This is the meaning of "form is emptiness."

Emptiness does not mean nothingness. Emptiness is able to contain all myriad things. It is said in the sutras, "True emptiness does not obstruct wondrous existence, and wondrous existence does not obstruct true emptiness." Emptiness is spirit, while form is matter. Within matter there is spirit, while spirit requires form in order to manifest. Therefore, form and emptiness are "two in one, one with two."

Is emptiness existent or nonexistent? If you believe it is nonexistent, consider the fact that the earth, mountains, and rivers all exist within emptiness. Emptiness is the nature shared by all phenomena and myriad forms are phenomena. Substantial nature and manifest nature are one and the same.

The unenlightened are attached to the notion that all phenomena truly exists. Because of this, they encounter obstacles everywhere and are unable to connect the substantial nature of phenomena and the emptiness of its nature.

Once one realizes that all phenomena have no self and the emptiness of dependent origination, one then understands that the Buddha mind is one's own mind. This is the meaning of the saying "My face is the Buddha face."

Awakened to the Wisdom
and Insight of Buddha

Chan Master Chìshān Fǎrěn was from the Chahar province, born around 1842 CE. He was recognized as one of the four great elders of the Chan School during the late Qing dynasty. Due to his practice from within a thatched hut on Mount Chì in Jùróng, Nanjing, he was given the honorific title, "The Elder of Red Mountain."

One day, the Elder of Red Mountain ascended to the hall and began teaching the Dharma saying, "My place here is an arena for selecting buddhas, turning you into dragons and elephants. This place is not here to allow people to idly eat, idly sleep, and idly doze off. Everyone, the essence of the *Lotus Sūtra* is to open up to awaken into the wisdom and insight of Buddhahood. Masters and patriarchs over the generations have already revealed its profound meanings, however, today I want to listen to your true wisdom and penetrating views from your own minds.

The Elder of Red Mountain immediately pointed downwards to his student Chan Master Chǔquán Quánzhèn saying, "Come, you speak first. Concerning this matter of 'opening up to awaken into the wisdom and insight of Buddhahood,' how should one go about this process of opening up?" Chan Master Chǔquán Quánzhèn could not come up with anything for an answer.

The Elder of Red Mountain immediately denounced him loudly yelling, "What have you been doing all this time? Do you think learning Chan is child's play? What areyou waiting for? Kneel in contemplation!"

After one incense stick's worth of practice time, the Elder of Red Mountain examined him again, "Speak, how does opening occur?"

The Elder of Red Mountain saw that Master Chǔquán Quánzhèn was still unable to answer. Again he erupted angrily, "When will you awaken through contemplation? Do it again!"

However, after the second stick of incense finished, Master Chǔquán Quánzhèn was still unable to find words.

The Elder of the Red Mountain refused his dismissal. With a stern voice and fierce expression he barked, "If you cannot 'open' today, then I will have you die here as you kneel in contemplation!"

Chan Master Chǔquán Quánzhèn's mind was anxious as though burning. Drops of sweat cascaded off of him like falling rain. Right after the third stick of incense had just finished, the rector raised his paddle and broke the silence with a loud "thwack!"

Chan Master Chǔquán Quánzhèn abruptly lit up inside his mind. He finally experienced a swift moment of awakening.

Beside him he heard the Elder of Red Mountain examining him once more, "How does one open up to awaken into the wisdom and insight of Buddhahood?"

With great confidence Chan Master Chǔquán Quánzhèn answered, "Just by awakening into the wisdom and insight of Buddhahood."

The Elder of Red Mountain could not help but laugh uproariously as he clapped his hands and spoke, "Excellent, Chǔquán. Today's three incense stick's worth of time spent kneeling was clearly not wasted."

The Elder of Red Mountain was a famous elder from the modern period. He resided and cultivated on Mount Chì in Nanjing. In the end, it was inside his dwelling hut that he finally saw the depth of the world within his body-mind. The Elder of Red Mountain instructed everyone that they were not allowed to eat idly or doze off idly, and that every day they should truly conduct their Dharma practice satisfactorily. Since education should have serious requirements, Chan Master Chǔquán Quánzhèn was made to kneel for three incense periods. This can be said to be an excellent demonstration of the Chan School.

As for the "wisdom and insight of Buddha," is it not the case that the Four Noble Truths, the Twelve Links of Dependent Origination, the Three Dharma Seals, worries, emptiness, impermanence, no-self, and other such teachings are the wisdom and insights of the Buddha?

Who are Our Descendants?

Chan Master Tiānhuáng Dàowù paid a visit to Chan Master Shítóu Xīqiān. As soon as he saw Chan Master Shítóu he asked, "May I please ask you, Master: aside from liberation, meditation, and wisdom, what other truths can you tell people?"

Chan Master Shítóu Xīqiān responded, "There have never been shackles of attachment here. What 'liberation' could I discuss with others?"

Clearly displeased, Chan Master Tiānhuáng remarked, "How are people supposed to understand you when you say things like that?"

Chan Master Shítóu asked, "Do you know about 'emptiness?'"

Chan Master Tiānhuáng answered, "I've had understanding on 'emptiness' for some time now! As the saying goes, 'True emptiness does not obstruct wondrous existence, and wondrous existence does not obstruct true emptiness.'"

Chan Master Shítóu sighed, "Oh... I didn't expect that you were also a person who came from over there (meaning the world of delusion)."

Chan Master Tiānhuáng quickly denied, "I am not from over there. In order to be an 'over there' there must be an 'over here.' Are you suggesting that I still carry traces of where I come from with me?"

Chan Master Shítóu Xīqiān answered, "I've known for long where you have come from."

Chan Master Tiānhuáng unhappily replied, "How can you make such an accusation without the slightest bit of evidence?"

Chan Master Shítóu laughed boisterously. He pointed at Chan Master Tiānhuáng and remarked, "Your body is the evidence. Is that not where you come from?"

Chan Master Tiānhuáng replied, "It may be said that the origin is where 'he' is from and this destination is where 'he' has gone. But what is it that we should ultimately teach our descendants?"

Unable to contain himself, Chan Master Shítóu cried out scolding, "So, who exactly are our descendants!?"

With that shout, Tiānhuáng experienced sudden great awakening.

Chan Master Shítóu Xīqiān and Chan Master Tiānhuáng Dàowù's discussion of 'over there' and 'over here,' was the discussion of samsara. "I know that you are from there" indicates that the individual is still lost in the delusion of living and dying. The so-called evidence is the karmic physical body which is subject to outflow.

After some deep contemplation, Chan Master Tiānhuáng admitted that he had not yet gained liberation. He declared, "... wherever 'he' comes from, or wherever 'he' goes;" meaning that he was no longer bound to the cycle of life and death. However, Chan Master Tiānhuáng expressed concern for descendants. Those from before and those who will come after, those who are born and those who will die. Worrying over these, how is he going to resolve life and death? It is no wonder that Chan Master Shítóu yelled at him, "Who are our descendants?"

Pick It Up!

Chan Master Xīnxīng Yányáng was a native of Xīnxīng, Wǔníng in Hóngzhōu (present day Jiāngxī) during the Tang dynasty. He was the Dharma heir of Chan Master Zhàozhōu Cóngshěn. Chan Master Zhàozhōu Cóngshěn was known as "Zhàozhōu Ancient Buddha." He resided at Guānyīn Monastery in Zhàozhōu, Héběi (present day Bólín Chan Temple) for forty years.

When Chan Master Xīnxīng Yányáng first met Chan Master Zhàozhōu Cóngshěn, he asked, "What should one do when nothing arises?"

Chan Master Zhàozhōu Cóngshěn looked at the young student monk before him. He thought, "For a student monk to declare that he has seen his own original face, this youngster is acting far too arrogantly."

As he was thinking this, Chan Master Zhàozhōu walked toward Chan Master Xīnxīng Yányáng. As the two passed one another, Zhàozhōu suddenly turned around and shouted into Chan Master Xīnxīng Yányáng's ear, "Let go!"

When Chan Master Xīnxīng Yányáng heard these words, he realized his error and humbled himself, "Since nothing arises, what am I supposed to let go of?"

Chan Master Zhàozhōu laughed heartily and answered, "Since you cannot let go, then you should pick it up."

Chan Master Xīnxīng Yányáng suddenly had a great awakening. He immediately bowed before Chan Master Zhàozhōu.

"Nothing arises" means that nothing is brought over. For the young Chan master had realized the Way, but he still had habitual tendencies which he could not hide before Zhàozhōu Ancient Buddha. When Chan Master Yányáng said "I am not bringing anything here," Chan Master Zhàozhōu followed up with, "Let go!" This was giving him a serious instruction, meaning: Have you let go of your arrogance? Have you let go of your conceit? Have you let go of your attachments? And can you even let go your realization of the Way?

Although young Yányáng understood Chan Master Zhàozhōu's message, nevertheless, he still replied, "Since nothing arises, what am I supposed to let go of?" Chan Master Zhàozhōu immediately replied, "Well, then pick it up!" Through this exchange with Chan Master Zhàozhōu, the young Chan practitioner finally experienced sudden awakening.

In Buddhism, we pick it up when things are useful and when it's no longer useful, we let it go. When we carry a heavy object around that is not useful, don't we feel it's encumbering?

Even though we have truly let go, when there is the need for compassion and the need to help others, we still have to pick it up!

Glossary

chiliocosm: Buddhist term for the universe.

deva: A heavenly being. Literally, meaning "being of light."

dhāraṇī: Also known as "mantra" or "spell." Literally, it means "uniting and holding," which further extends to "uniting all dharmas and holding all meanings."

Dharma realm: It indicates the notion of true nature that encompasses all phenomena. As a space or realm of dharmas, it is the uncaused and immutable totality in which all phenomena arise, abide, and extinguish.

Gathas: A verse or poem

gōng'àns: Dialogues or stories in Chan Buddhism, often between Chan masters and practitioners.

huàtóu: Short phrases for contemplation in Chan practice.

kalpa: An Indic unit of time measurement. A kalpa is an incalculably long period of time spanning the creation and destruction of the universe

kāṣāya: Buddhist monastic robes

King Yama: The god of death and lord of the underworld.

ksana: Buddhist term describing a moment; the smallest possible unit of time.

Māra: A malevolent being that embodies desire and is an adversary of the Buddha. The name is also used to refer to mental qualities that impede spiritual progress.

Mount Sumeru: The central world-mountain in Buddhist cosmology.

Mind-Only: Also "Consciousness Only." One of two primary Mahayana schools that developed in India and asserted that all phenomena originate from the consciousness.

parinirvāṇa: Final nirvana. This phrase often refers to the physical death of the Buddha, when all his ties to karma were completely severed.

Saha World: Literally, "land of endurance." It indicates the present world where we reside, which is full of suffering to be endured.

samadhi: A very high level of meditative concentration, defined as "one-pointed" concentration or composure of the mind.

saṃsāra: The cycle of repeated birth and death.

sastra: Commentaries or treatises on the Buddha's teachings.

Skanda: General Skanda, a guardian or protector of Buddhist temples and monasteries.

sutra: The recorded discourses or teachings of the Buddha.

vinaya: Indicating precepts, rules, and disciples.

vajra: Sword or "diamond"

About the Author

Venerable Master Hsing Yun was born in Jiangsu Province, China in 1927. He has studied at various renowned Buddhist institutions such as Qixia Vinaya College and Jiaoshan Buddhist College.

Soon after his arrival in Taiwan in 1949, he became the chief editor of Human Life, a Buddhist magazine. In 1952, his efforts in establishing Buddhist Chanting Groups strengthened the foundation for his subsequent endeavors in the promotion of the Dharma. The Master founded Fo Guang Shan Monastery in 1967, with the primary goal of promoting Humanistic Buddhism through Buddhist education, culture, charity, and propogation of the Dharma. Since then, over two hundred branch temples have been established in major cities around the world. He has also set up art galleries, libraries, publishing houses, bookstores, mobile clinics Buddhist colleges and universities including University of the West, Fo Guang University, Nan Hua University, Nan Tien Institute and Guang Ming College. In 1977, the Fo Guang Tripitika Editorial Board was formed to compile the Fo Guang Buddhist Canon and the Fo Guang Dictionary of Buddhism. Many other works in Buddhism have also been published.

Master Hsing Yun has dedicated his life to propogating Humanistic Buddhism. As a global citizen, he continues to foster joy and harmony, oneness and coexistence, respect and tolerance, and equality and peace throughout the world. When he founded the Buddha's Light International Association in 1991 and was elected president of its world headquarters, he was closer to realizing the ideal of having "the Buddha's light shining throughout the three thousand realms, and the Dharma water flowing across the five continents."

About Buddha's Light Publications

Ever since he became a Buddhist monk, Venerable Master Hsing Yun has strongly believed that books and other documentation of the Buddha's teachings unite us spiritually, allowing us to reach a higher level of Buddhist practice, and continuously challenge our definition of our lives.

In 1996, the Fo Guang Shan International Translation Ceneter was established to fulfill this purpose. This marked the beginning of a string of publications translated into various languages from the Master's original writings in Chinese. In 2001, Buddha's Light Publishing was founded to further facilitate this progress. Presently, several translation centers have been set up worldwide. Centers located in Los Angeles, USA; Sydney, Australia; Berlin, Germany; Argentina; South Africa; and Japan coordinate to complete and distribute translation or publication projects across the globe. In 2015, the publishing house was reorganized as Buddha's Light Publications, USA Corp.; continuing the Fo Guang Shan International Translation Center mission of publishing translated Buddhist books and other valuable works. Buddha's Light Publications is committed to building bridges between East and West, Buddhist communities, and cultures. All proceeds from our book sales support Buddhist propogation efforts.